LIKE W...

Rita F. Snowden is widely known in many countries and is the author of more than sixty books for adults and children. After six years at business she trained as a deaconess of the New Zealand Methodist Church, serving in turn two pioneer country areas before moving to the largest city for several years of social work during an economic depression.

Miss Snowden has served the world Church, beyond her own denomination, with regular broadcasting commitments. She has written and spoken in Britain, Canada, the United States, in Australia, and in Tonga at the invitation of Queen Salote. She has represented her church at the World Methodist Conference in Oxford; later being elected the first woman Vice-President of the New Zealand Methodist Church, and President of its Deaconess Association. She is an Honorary Vice-President of the New Zealand Women Writers' Society, a Fellow of the International Institute of Art and Letters, and a member of P.E.N.

Miss Snowden has been honoured by the award of the Order of the British Empire, and by the citation of "The Upper Room" in America.

Her most recent books are *Prayers for Busy People, Christianity Close to Life, Bedtime Stories and Prayers* (for children), *I Believe Here and Now, Discoveries That Delight, Further Good News, Continually Aware, Good Company* and *Prayers in Large Print*.

Rita F. Snowden

LIKE WIND ON THE GRASSES

"The wind is blowing, I am refreshed."
Archbishop Anthony Bloom

Collins
FOUNT PAPERBACKS

First published in Great Britain in 1986
by Fount Paperbacks, London

Copyright © Rita F. Snowden 1986

Made and printed in Great Britain by
William Collins Sons & Co. Ltd, Glasgow

For my English Friend
Joy

Contents

Acknowledgements

The author and publisher are grateful to use in this book the following material from other writers:

Dannie Abse, *A Poet in the Family*, Hutchinson.

James Agate, *Ego 9*, George Harrap & Co. Ltd.

Dr William Barclay, review of *Canon Peter Green* and other material used by permission.

G. F. Bradby, "Teach Me to Know" in *Through the Christian Year*, arranged by G. F. Bradby and J. W. Hunkin, SCM Press.

Dr Alan Brash, in a "Faith for Today" programme broadcast by New Zealand Broadcasting Corporation.

Shona Caughey, in a radio script broadcast by N.Z.B.C..

Ellen Frances Gilbert, in *Short Prayers for a Long Day*, ed. by Giles and Melville Harcourt, Collins Liturgical.

Muriel Grainger, "The Apple Tree" (unpublished).

Asa Johnson, "It must have happened" (unpublished).

Father James Lyons, in a radio script broadcast by N.Z.B.C..

Ruth Pidwell, in a radio script broadcast by N.Z.B.C..

Alistair MacLean, "We are not puppets" in *The Quiet Heart*, Allenson & Co. Ltd, London.

Bernard Mobbs, *Rebel Emotions*, Hodder & Stoughton.

Ernest Raymond, *In the Steps of St Francis*, Rich and Cavan.

Jim Skett, in a radio script broadcast by N.Z.B.C..

Dr J. S. Stewart, *The Wind of the Spirit*, Hodder & Stoughton.

Dr J. S. Stewart, *The Life and Teaching of Jesus Christ*, St Andrew Press, Edinburgh.

David Watson, *I Believe in the Church*, Hodder & Stoughton.

Introduction

It's not always easy to put life's most treasurable experiences into words. Do you sometimes find yourself at a loss?

> Leaping forth from the loins of these
>   comfortable hills,
> a young wind refreshes me as nothing else,
> sweeping away loose things as it wills,
> weaving with joy through these grasses –
>   cleansing, quickening
> all with courage to stand in this place,
> or to sing like this poplar;
> matching the mind's high plateau
>   with life's delight,
> blowing where it listeth, out of man's
>   sight,
> in the manner of His lasting Spirit.
>
> R. F. S.

I can't imagine a world with endless calm holding sway – with no movement in the grasses, the trees, no ripples on the lakes; I find it hard to believe that God would be satisfied with that kind of world. Early on, the Psalmist – rejoicing in the world God made – said of Him: "*He bringeth the wind out of his treasuries*" (Psalm 135:7). Centuries later, Jesus drew attention to the wind. Said He: "*The wind bloweth where it listeth, and thou hearest the sound thereof, but canst not tell whence it cometh, and whither it goeth; so is every one that is born of the Spirit*" (John 3:8).

My Scottish friend, Dr J. S. Stewart, scholar-preacher-writer, uses the word "impalpable" in reference to it – "imperceptible to the touch"; "not easily grasped by the mind" (as the Oxford Dictionary puts it. And I can't think of a better statement): "To everyone brought up in the Jewish tradition, it was natural, almost inevitable, *to compare the Spirit with the Wind.*"

It was not, from the beginning, a negative thing – far from it – rather a glorious, positive energy, an exhilaration: "The word *ruach* stood in fact for three things. It meant breath, that most impalpable part of existence, the breath of life. It meant also the desert wind, tearing violently across the land with primal energy and elemental force. *And it meant the Spirit of God, the supernatural power that sweeps across the ages, and bursts into history, and takes possession of the lives of men.*"

It was in the last-named sense that the New Testament Book of Acts, at a loss for earth words to record one of the greatest happenings, set it down like this: "When the day of Pentecost was fully come, they [the early followers of our Lord] were all with one accord in one place. And suddenly there came a sound from heaven as of a rushing mighty wind" (Acts 2:1–2). (But it wasn't only a moment of rare emotion, as all too many today seem content to count it.) As Dr Stewart reminds us in his book, *The Wind of the Spirit,* "Always there are unmistakable signs when the Spirit goes to work . . . When a man once weak and shifty and unreliable becomes strong and clean and victorious; when a church once stagnant and conventional and introverted throws off its dull tedium and catches fire and becomes alert and missionary-minded; when Christians of different denominations begin to realize there is more in the Risen Christ to unite them than there can be anywhere else in the world or in their own traditions to divide them; when religion, too long taboo in polite conversation, becomes a talking point again; when decisions for Christ are seen worked out in family and business relationships; when mystic vision bears fruit in social passion – then indeed, the world is made to know that something is happening." In other words, he is saying, the place where newness begins is in one's surrendered personality – showing clearly in those lovely qualities Paul listed as "fruits of the Spirit: love, joy, peace, longsuffering, gentleness, goodness, faith, meekness, temperance" (Galatians 5:22–23).

For a brief time, this world saw all these qualities in Christ. Then those closest heard Him say: "It is expedient for you that I go away: for if I go not away, the Comforter [the Spirit, that our modern translations render 'the Helper'] will not come unto you; *but if I depart, I will send him unto you*" (John 16:7; Moffatt's New Testament; Dr William Barclay's New Testament; and the Good News Bible). The very nature of this earth life is one of physical limitations. There must have been other highways (besides that one where blind Bartimaeus sat with his begging bowl) to which the earthly Christ could not come with the gift of new sight; other distraught mothers like the widow of Nain, following her dead boy's bier; other much-visited homes where He might have known hospitality, besides that of Martha, Mary and their brother Lazarus. But whilst His Incarnation meant much, *it had its limitations*; in Dr Westcott's remembered words: "The withdrawal of the limited bodily presence necessarily prepared the way for the recognition of a Universal Presence." To make this glorious reality doubly clear, Dr Gore's words are: "The coming of the Holy Spirit was not merely to supply the absence of the Son, *but to complete His presence*."

So, in very truth, in this earth life of ours, we can sing:

11

O breath of God, breathe on us now,
 And move within us while we pray:
The spring of our new life art Thou,
 The very light of our new day.

O strangely art Thou with us, Lord,
 Neither in height nor depth to seek;
In nearness shall Thy voice be heard;
 Spirit to spirit Thou dost speak.

* * *

No earth-setting is too simple for the introduction of this great experience.

I have circled the earth several times, but I don't need to go that far to happen upon a reminder of this. A few steps from my own front door will serve, and in any season. There, beyond grasses, the road leads off into far distant places. "When I hear people say that they have not found the world so interesting as to be in love with it," said Hudson, the English naturalist, "I am apt to think they have never seen it, *not even a blade of grass*."

What would he have said of those of us here who fail to appreciate His great gift of life, "like wind on the grasses"?

Jesus loved grasses. One day, He fed five thousand, seated upon them in gaily garmented groups. The gospel says: "There was much grass in the place" (John 6:10). They must have looked like gay flower beds against that green – men, women, youths and little children! It's a delight to picture the scene.

On another occasion, our Lord, as teacher, was heard to say: "If God so clothe the grass of the field . . . shall He not much more clothe you, O ye of little faith?" (Matthew 6:30). *Nothing of God's generous giving was too commonplace for Him.*

12

Much nearer to us in time, one of our poets drew attention to this:

> Christ talked of grass, and wind, and rain,
>   And fig trees, and fine weather,
> And made it His delight to bring
>   Heaven and Earth together.

Though many today fail to see God the Creator through Nature's commonplaces – none of us can afford not to. The teaching of our sensitive Lord and Master is so continually full, as you must have noticed. His humble listeners, as well as the officers of the Chief Priests and Pharisees, sent amongst the listening crowds to trap Him, could only say with complete agreement, "Never man spake like this man" (John 7:46). Not that He was the first or sole teller of parables centred on commonplace happenings. The art of setting *living truth in a pattern of the familiar* had long been a means of teaching. There were examples in the Old Testament of which Jesus, growing up, must have been aware (2 Samuel 12:1–14; Isaiah 5:1–7; Ezekiel 17:1–10). A smattering of others was to be found in rabbinical literature, reaching up through 300 BC to AD 200.

Jesus did not need to invent this method of teaching – He found it already long and widely used – but He was a rare master at it. "He made it", as Dr Hugh Martin, one of our modern authorities, delights to say, "something new. And He used it, because the realm of Nature was to Him a sacrament of things divine."

If those of us, to whom His teaching filtered down with the passing of the centuries, had been ready to accept His lead, much of our time's painful conflict between Religion and Science would have been avoided. Now, happily, that does not as deeply hinder things, as once it did.

One lovely thing was the way Jesus spoke to *both men*

and women, because He saw that each, in God's holy purpose, shared life – and needed to share truth. His respect for persons was in no wise limited to one sex. This, in His time, was a far more remarkable stance than many of us recognize today. On occasion, of course, He spoke especially to the oft-forgotten women, as when He chose to mention the patching of clothes, or referred to a woman who had lost a coin. He talked about breadmaking, with its essential leaven, and He carried forward into His ministry what He had observed in His growing years with His mother Mary, in Nazareth.

To borrow Dorothy Sayers' splendid way of putting it: "They had never known a man like this Man – there had never been such another. A prophet and teacher Who never nagged at them, never flattered or coaxed or patronized; Who never made arch jokes about them, never treated them either as 'the women, God help us!' or 'the ladies, God bless them!' Who rebuked without querulousness and praised without condescension; Who took their questions and arguments seriously; Who never mapped out their spheres for them, never urged them to be feminine or jeered at them for being female."

Little wonder the women saw in His teaching what they did. There was no part of life that could be dismissed as wholly secular – even the use of salt in the preservation of family food, of flesh and fish, and the pleasant savouring of it. This must have been shared between Mary and Joseph. The talk about ploughs, and foolish builders who raised a house on sand only to find that it collapsed, may have grown out of talk with Joseph. Jesus entered into the wholeness of life; He rejoiced in God's gifts offered so freely to minister to body, mind and spirit. St Mark has a telling word or two: "As Jesus passed by, *He saw* . . ." "What?" you may ask. The answer is: the beauty of wild flowers, the birds above the fields, the threatening storm disturbing the mother hen and her brood. "And whom?" –

children at their games; weddings and funerals; life in the market; Levi, sitting at his receipt of custom, sick of the futility of it; Mary Magdalene of the streets, seeking some meaning in her life. Nothing escaped Him. *As He passed by, He saw . . . Not even the commonplace use of wind on the grasses escaped Him.*

Bernard Mobbs takes pleasure in reminding us of this in our own day. In his little book, *Rebel Emotions* (Hodder & Stoughton, p. 118), "Rosalind Chalmers", he says, "was a polio victim and spent many months in hospital. She movingly described her feelings on the first occasion when she was brought down from her upstairs ward and viewed the hospital lawn at close quarters again. 'We stopped, and I stared at it in astonishment and exaltation', said she. 'Its greenness was of a quality beyond memory, and beyond imagination. I drank it in, and it was as if my body had *lacked some mysterious chlorophyll of its own*, which it now recognized and absorbed. That moment should be put in the scales against all the previous pain and frustration and humiliation.'"

And His wind on His grasses is one of His continuing ways of speaking to us each *with a life-long need to know His Spirit*!

Caring Counts!

As the colours of things around me on Sunday evenings sink with the sun, and birds fly homeward on tired wings, I often find myself enriched with a new kind of gratitude for life.

On the Sunday just past, it was so. My English friend Joy came as my guest to Sunday dinner and, as we sat later over our coffee, we found ourselves talking of certain values.

In ancient times, it seems, *people and things* often got mixed up. It was that way in Greece and Rome. Aristotle, the great Greek philosopher in pre-Christian times, actually said, "Master and slave have nothing in common: *a slave is a living tool, just as a tool is an inanimate slave*." And tragedy, of course, resulted, as it always will where it is forgotten that people are to be loved, and things are to be used – not the other way round.

Any Roman father, to instance but one example of these mixed-up values, could without question destroy a babe at birth. After a first girl, imperial Rome, anxious always about its army, required a father to bring up only healthy males. The rest were thrown out or, at best, sold as slaves to be "mere things".

At this point in our talk, my friend Joy surprisingly quoted one of my favourite sayings of that great Christian, von Hügel: "*Christianity taught us to care. Caring is the greatest thing. Caring matters most*." It's a gracious Christian truth, and an essential one; and to hear it upon my friend's lips gave me pleasure. It reminded me of a magazine cutting I had, and I rose to fetch it from my study.

It was a tribute to Joy's one-time minister in Eastbourne, and I had tucked it away among the good doctor's own writings that I treasured. Dr James Reid was widely known; and, when he died, the Rev. G. T. Bellhouse, the youngish minister who was to carry on much of his work, paid him this tribute: "He often used to say that the mark of a Christian was that he 'cared'; and *he* cared, and in times of trouble was the tenderest of pastors. I know what he meant to my own wife in her last testing week. Every visit to her left her braver and surer." And he counted it a rare privilege, he said, to be paying that tribute in that crowded church which they had both loved, St Andrew's, Eastbourne. The old doctor died on his eighty-sixth birthday.

Joy had known him long before I first met her – a meeting which came about through a relationship of Christian caring on both sides of the world. My friend Rene and I shared the pleasure of leading a fellowship in our home, once a fortnight. It was made up, at first, of young business women from nearby churches, but in time others from across the city asked if they might come. We were a happy company. The newspapers and radio kept us fully aware of what was happening on the other side of the world: the war was on – had been for some time – and many in Britain were hard pressed to meet day-to-day needs. We decided we would like to do something to help, and I undertook to get the address of an English church. The address, when it came, was that of St Andrew's, Eastbourne. I can't remember how many parcels we sent off, or how long we kept it up. I was the packer, and the parcels we made up were of all shapes, weights and sizes.

It was one early evening after the war had ended that I heard a knock at our front door. Rene was still engaged with her last music pupil, and I rose from my study chair to answer the door. There before me, in the light of that Summer evening, stood a young woman, who gave her

17

name and said she was from Eastbourne, in the south of England. She had come to say thank you for the parcels! And that was how we first met Joy; she had belonged to St Andrew's Church, and had now come out to our country as a nurse. (Hers was a very caring spirit too.)

The years went by, and she came often to our home – not by the front door any more, but by the back; into the kitchen perhaps, to cook up a fruit cake, as time and supplies allowed; or she came to stay the night in our spare bedroom. After some years, our friend returned to England, and on one of my journeys there we walked the Sussex Downs together and poked into her favourite villages. Later she returned to our country, and in time her mother joined her and set up home here, to which we were always welcome.

Years passed, and now Joy is once more on her own, following her mother's death. And I am on my own, following Rene's death. So we naturally get together occasionally for a meal, and there is always good talk, and renewing laughter.

So it was this Sunday, and I took the opportunity to ask some questions and to bring out my treasured cutting, "A Tribute to Dr James Reid". She was interested. "You knew him well, didn't you?" I asked, "more than just the fact that he was the minister of St Andrew's?"

"Oh, yes!" she replied, as I knew she would. He had been blind for a long time, and she added, "I used to go and read to him."

"How often?" I asked.

"Oh, about twice a week."

"Let me read you the rest of the tribute", I suggested. I'd sat fingering it for some time.

"Yes, do", my friend replied.

So I continued reading: "Of course, there is the natural sadness of parting with one we have known and loved so long; the feeling that a great support has been removed.

18

But we do not mourn as those without hope, and when we think of Dr Reid it is all thanksgiving for a long, rich life that meant so much to us, and to many all over the English-speaking world.

"He was one of the greatest preachers of our day, and there is hardly a minister's study anywhere without at least one or two of his books. He came to be known as 'Reid of Eastbourne', and ministers and lay people of all denominations crowded this church to hear him . . . He was never preaching for five minutes before he was dealing with some human situation, and dealing with it in such a way as to lead to victory.

"Of course, his own victory over his blindness, which precluded his ever reading for himself, added to his power. *He remained extraordinarily alert in mind, sensitive to the mood of the day, to every new leading of God's Spirit.* But in the services he conducted, it was not only the sermons people remembered, it was also the prayers. They seemed to lead straight into the secret place of the Most High.

"Many of us, too, remember him as pastor and friend. [And here comes the passage I've quoted already, but it is worth repeating.] He often used to say that the mark of a Christian was that he 'cared', and *he* cared . . . He was a great servant, not just of this church, but of this town. He saw the church, not as some seem to see it, just as an organization for the religious, but as the servant of the world . . . Much of the wider work done in this community was due to his leading and inspiration. And it was very fitting that on his retirement the Freedom of this Borough should have been conferred upon him.

"I remember his once telling me how a very intelligent woman had come to see him, saying that she could not believe in God; could he help her? They talked for some time, and as she left she said, 'I don't know that I yet believe in God, *but I do believe in you.*'

19

"You could not help but believe in James Reid: he was so real, so honest, so understanding, and through his faith, many learned to find a faith of their own."

It is a wonderful thing to be, like him, associated in people's minds, at the end of the day, at the end of the way, as "a caring person", following Christ.

Welcome!

One of the loveliest words in our speech is the word "Welcome". And its meaning, according to my Oxford Dictionary, supports it: "*Hail, know that your coming gives pleasure!*"

I know of no other word to match it, whether it be used between oneself and another over the doorstep, or more officially, in a communal or civic sense.

From time to time, we turn out to receive the Queen and the Duke of Edinburgh, the Prince of Wales and his Princess, or some other notable – our city or township be-flagged. And there is no mistaking the warmth and sincerity of that welcome.

Americans are particularly lavish – I was going to say "good" – at this. Maybe you have been in one of their cities when a procession comes through. After a wait that seems endlessly long, there is a waving of flags, a calling of "Welcome!" and a dropping of ticker-tape and confetti from their high city windows. It's fun, for all of us, and provides a memorable and colourful sight.

Then almost as suddenly as it began, it's over – the crowd spills back across the cleared space and, excitement reduced, it's time to go. The day Colonel John Glenn – after his famous flight into outer space – rode in procession along Broadway in New York, a reporter said, "It was the greatest ever!" Then he had soon to admit that the city's street-cleaning department, in collecting up the coloured papers that had fluttered down, had faced an unparalleled task. He claimed that the welcome "weighed three thousand four hundred and seventy-four tons". (That struck me as a very strange way to reckon up a welcome – to weigh it! Can a welcome be weighed?)

* * *

We all have our own ways of expressing welcome, and that is how it should be. For life here could not richly proceed without it, either personally or communally.

Yet I must say that it astonishes me that the Bible, being so close to life, does not, in our loved Authorized Version, find room for the word "Welcome" in its pages. (We have to wait for Moffatt's more modern version for that – and there it is freely and gloriously used, beginning away back in Genesis 9:27: "May God enlarge Japheth! May he *be welcome* in the tents of Shem!" And the lovely word is thereafter sprinkled right through the Old Testament and on up into the New.)

* * *

I find the word "Welcome" early in John's gospel (chapter 1:10–11; Moffatt), but there it is part of a statement that carries all the pathos in the world: "He [Christ Jesus] entered the world which existed through Him – yet the world did not recognize Him; He came to what was His own, *yet His own folk did not welcome Him.*"

We know, and have known since childhood, how there was no worthy crib prepared for His birth. And quite soon, as Christmas approaches year by year, another spate of cards comes through the post, reminding us of this vital piece of history: a census time, and a journey to Bethlehem.

The people had long toyed with the promise of His coming, foretold by the prophets, but somehow they had got it wrong. As our poet, George MacDonald, reminds us tellingly:

22

Welcome!

They all were looking for a king
  To slay their foes and lift them high;
Thou cam'st a little baby thing
  That made a woman cry.

So there was no welcome – only a casual place in an outbuilding of an inn, a bed of straw where cattle found shelter and food; and soon the unexpected lot of a little refugee and His earth family, escaping through the night from the anger of Herod.

But in time, of course, Herod died, and the small family came back to the village of Nazareth, to a modest carpenter's home, and occupation.

* * *

There followed a period of eager growth. The New Testament says very beautifully: "And Jesus increased in wisdom [mentally] and in stature [physically], and in favour with God [spiritually] and man [socially]" (Luke 2:52; Moffatt). The result was a four-square balanced personality!

Then God's call came to Him, to a larger, more costly ministry. After forty days of meditating and testing alone in the desert, He came again to Nazareth, and there in the place of worship He rose to speak to the people. But there was no welcome that day. (Read about it afresh in Luke 4:14 27; Moffatt).

But as Dr J. S. Stewart's little book *The Life and Teaching of Jesus Christ* (reissued by the Saint Andrew Press, Edinburgh) underlines, the truth we must not miss: *not everyone rejected Jesus when He came.*

"The Evangelists record *the welcome of His mother*. That mother's love", as Dr Stewart adds reverently, "was the nearest thing to His own . . . Out of all the women in the world, God chose Mary to make the home in which

23

the world's Redeemer should be reared. It was at Mary's knee that Jesus lisped His first childhood prayers . . . She was lonely in the sublime destiny for which God appointed her; lonely in the deep thoughts she kept and pondered in her heart; lonely on the morning when Jesus left His boyhood home, and turned His face to the world; loneliest of all on the day when 'there stood by the cross, his mother' (John 19:25). But," Dr Stewart has to add, "there shines out also her glad self-sacrifice: 'Be it unto me according to thy word' (Luke 1:38), as she responded to God with a rare willingness. And even when the sword, of which Simeon was to speak, was piercing, her spirit could still exult in the beauty and strength and holiness of the Son whom God had given her."

Early there was also, as we all know, *the welcome of the shepherds*, *the welcome of the wise men*, and later *the welcome of Simeon and Anna*. All these are realities good to remember. Then there was *the welcome of John the Baptist*: "Looking upon Jesus as he walked, he saith, 'Behold the Lamb of God!'" (John 1:36). Afterwards came *the welcome of Andrew* and, next day, *that of Simon*, followed by *that of Philip* and *Nathanael*.

In John 4:4–30 is recorded *the welcome of an unknown woman at a well*, who gave Him water when He thirsted – a woman to whom no one else, in her own need, ever gave a welcome. And there were *the humble mothers of Salem, with their little children* (Mark 10:13–15).

It's a joy to go through the gospels, turning page after page, searching out these records of welcome. (Take time to do it!) It would be a shame to miss out *the little Bethany home of Mary, Martha and Lazarus*, where Jesus found the door always on the latch. And there was the upper room in the great heartless city of Jerusalem, where Jesus shared His Last Supper before He died, a place generally thought to have been *the home of Mark's mother*. And there was the resurrection welcome which followed, at *the home of two travellers* with whom Jesus walked to Emmaus (Luke 24:13–35) – and our hearts warm every time we turn to the record of it, as when we sing one of our best-known hymns, "Abide with me!"

So this wonderful reality comes close to our earth life, and we would be poor without it. It is here and now a pleasure to pause, and to recall outstanding instances in our own experience – as Jesus must have recalled those we have mentioned, and others, during His life here.

On one of my travels, I remember thankfully coming, late and tired, to a certain Christian home I had not visited before. The warm light of the hall when the door was opened to my knock was not more real than the loving welcome that wrapped me round. The table was set, though the children had had their meal and were in comfortable positions before the fire. After I had eaten, we clustered there together to share a bedtime game of dominoes.

Next morning, I was let into a secret. "Ruth is a funny wee dear", said the mother of that family. "Every night, when she says her prayers, she tells God the things that have happened during the day. Last night, whilst you continued at the fireside with my husband, I slipped upstairs to see the children safely tucked in, and I overheard Ruth at her prayers: 'Oh, yes, and there's another thing. We've got Sister Rita Snowden staying with us. We're allowed to call her "Sister Rita" – it's quite all right – but her real name is Rita F. Snowden. *It's on her books – you can see it.*'"

Delightful! In that instant I knew that the welcome I'd received was not only a matter of earth, but something which concerned our Father in heaven, as well. And perhaps, between Christians, that's the thing about true welcomes – they always do!

This secret, of course, has nothing to do with geography, language or colour – it can happen anywhere, as it happened to our Lord. Palestine was not a big country, as geographers tellingly remind us, and some of us will never forget it, having travelled it from end to end and from side to side. For that matter, my own country is not a big one either. One overseas woman, looking at its little piece of red on the world map, wrote to ask me exactly where on it I lived: "Perhaps by that very large lake in the middle of the north is your home, or else on the seashore?" I had to reply that, despite the appearance of the map, there is nevertheless a surprising area of land here where we are happy to live.

And this word "Welcome" means something very real to us. In thanksgiving for knowledge of it, I wrote these lines:

> As one of Time's travellers,
>   I give thanks to God,
> That I have friends with clear eyes
>   And life-giving laughter,
> *And doors on the latch*
>   *That spell "Welcome!"*
>
> R. F. S.

I'll Never Forget It!

I shared in a miracle today, and I've been thinking about it ever since – it was to me so pleasurable, and so unexpected. For the first time, I was visiting the home of my friends David and Enid. When their young son, Peter, was born, although I sent them a card of family congratulations, because their little town, beautiful though it is, lies some distance off the bus route, I had not since managed to get out to see them. Even today, of course, David was away at business, and I was sorry about that. He should have been there with us, to rejoice in the unforgettable happening. But I'm sure he and Enid will not cease talking about it for a long time to come. Today young Peter *took his first step in this world!* And I was there to witness it!

An old proverb, all but forgotten, suddenly danced out of my memory: "*The longest journey begins with the first step!*" Here and there, in many homes, of course, young children are daily doing this miraculous thing – taking a first step that will, all being well, take them into interesting and beautiful places. And young Peter today began on this great adventure.

So far, it is centred on the sitting room carpet, and attended by a certain sense of insecurity. But that will pass. Soon, he will be finding his way to the front gate, to the letter box fastened on to the gatepost, to which the Postie comes daily. And then to the grocer's, half a mile off – an essential and neighbourly undertaking, for both Peter and his mother.

The years will pass – five of them, at least – and he will be waving his mother goodbye at that little gate, and setting off down the road to school. He will be learning to open books wisely, to look at pictures – and to read. And when he comes back home, each night he will repeat nursery rhymes that will trip off his tongue with pride – and one by one they will lead him on to endless delight.

Then he will mix with playmates and, with the passing of the days and years, will make new friends. There will be songs to sing, and music to play, listen to, and dance to; and fascinating things to make, for hands, like feet, are wonderful. As the years slip by, the world will need what Peter can do with the skills that reside in *his* hands. By that time in his life's journey, that began with his first step today, he may, among the fine things he learns at college, chance on a favourite saying of a modern dramatist: "If one had never seen a hand," said Christopher Fry, "and were suddenly presented for the first time with this strange· and wonderful thing, what a magnificently shocking and inexplicable and mysterious thing it would be." (Some nice long words to roll off the tongue – but by this time on his journey Peter will have gathered for himself a fair idea of what they mean. And he will know that, for all the machines in this world in which he is called to live, travel and serve, there are things that *only hands* can do: pick a flower, catch a fish in a stream, plant a tree that will live on after he has gone far on his journey. He will hear others saying, "Lend a hand" and know what it means; he might even come to the point where, like David his father, he finds himself talking of "having his hands full"; or he may come to a lecture room to cast his vote, when some adult issue needs "a show of hands". Four fingers and a thumb, twice multiplied, only God could invent: it is one of His many earth miracles – sensitive yet strong, each opening and closing in creativeness; continually reaching out in generosity, compassion, service.)

In his young men's class, or at church, he will almost certainly run upon the challenging saying of the Young Master of Life, about hands and feet – "setting his hand to the plough" – and it will have graphic meaning for him. "No man," it will tell him, "having put his hand to the plough, and looking back, is fit for the kingdom of God" (Luke 9:62). *This is something vastly more than "a journey" involving body and mind – it is an adventure of spirit.* And a man can't make sense of any part of his long journey in this fascinating life *without linking all together!*

* * *

Peter's God-given hands and feet will be linked in all his undertakings! It may indeed be that "the longest journey begins with the first step", but there are many steps called for, after that, and some of them may lead him into steep and unpromising places. He may not always speak of all of them, as he daily mingles with men and women in high and responsible places; but there are many ways of getting to know what a man's journey through this world means to him, and what his values are. There is a strange little verse in the Book of Proverbs (6:13; A.V.) which says of a man as human as Peter will be: "*He speaketh with his feet!*" In other words, watch where he goes – to church, to committee rooms and board rooms where worthwhile decisions are taken, to council chambers, and centres of government, where far-reaching and costly projects are considered, for the sake of rich and poor, both in his own land and in others.

For Peter, by then, will realize that *he must be a world citizen*, honouring God in his offering of service. And that challenge faces us each, once we start to walk about the world. One of the most telling prayers we can share is by someone satisfied simply to call himself "Anonymous". It says, as honestly as any one of us can speak:

My Father,
I walk in a world where beauty is,
and song, and many a joy;
where mystery halts my thought,
and sorrow keeps her court.
I cannot walk safely unless *Thou hold my hand,
and guide my feet.*

From Dullness . . . Deliver Us!

It was the sort of morning I like to remember – the air fresh, and the little country stream beside which I was staying, flowing sweetly. On a branch above eye level was a bird. There was no missing him – about seven inches long, a massive head and fine practical beak: a kingfisher. So colourful was he! His upper parts presented a glorious blue, with a greenish gloss on his crown and wings. A little white patch was under his chin and on each side of his neck, and he finished off with a stubby tail. Only later came his shrill call: "*Chee!*" or "*Chi-kee!*" He was clearly a fellow intent on business. All too soon, he was to me but a spectacular streak speeding downstream.

I find myself easily referring to him in the masculine sense, perhaps because of his command. I have no knowledge of his mate, save that I am told their chosen nest is a hole about a yard in length, reaching into a sandy bank. The nesting chamber is likely to be strewn with dried fishbones, on which the eggs will be laid. S. Vere Benson, a bird watcher, writing in *The Observer Book of Birds*, says of the eggs: "There will be six to eight . . . white, and rather round."

But it is the kingfisher's colour scheme that wins my heart. And there is always, I am glad to say, the possibility of spotting him in parts of my own country, as well as above the streams, rivers and lakes of Britain. In an English countryside book to which I often turn, *Content With What I Have*, C. Henry Warren tells of several other bird watchers who rejoice in the colours of the kingfisher. He introduces one by name: Mrs Drage who, moving from the town to the country, finds it "an adventure, a

31

constant source of discovery". (I can understand that.)
"Mrs Drage", he continues, "has turned into a real
walker, and her chief delights are the birds she never
tires of watching. Even the sparrows that nest in her
thatch are a joy to her."

I don't have a thatched cottage myself, although I do
have a constant bunch of sparrows in my life – and I love
them for their perkiness, even though they have so little
colour. And it seems that sparrows everywhere are like
this. When I was in Jerusalem, I saw their kin in holes in
the ancient walls, and Jesus must have seen them there,
on His visits to the city, for He spoke of them as being
sold in the marketplace, as food for the poor: "two for a
farthing", or, if one had coins for a bargain, "five for two
farthings" (Matthew 10:29; Luke 12:6). (It was not that
Jesus was momentarily confused; each little bird, plucked
and offered as food in the marketplace, was of such little
worth that an *extra one*, now and again, could be thrown
in for nothing.)

Walking one day in a back street in Jerusalem, I
bought from a working potter a little flat dish, with a
single sparrow showing on it. It hangs now on my study
wall, constantly in view as I lift my eyes from my desk,
and I'm glad of that. I wouldn't have bought it, perhaps,
without our Lord's reference to the sparrow – a reference
made even though there is no splash of colour there.
That waits for the kingfisher, as Mrs Drage discovered.
"Recently," says Mr Warren, "she arrived at the library
agog with the information that she had been watching a
kingfisher, as she was leaning over a bridge. 'My
husband says it's rare', she announced excitedly. 'Is it
really?'"

"Rare or not," adds Mr Warren, "it had roused her
heart *like a poem*."

I can understand that, for I have just begun one of my
own:

Poised on a branch of advantage against the sky,
the kingfisher watches acutely each fish and fly
moving within pool and weed –
then shows himself fashioned of sapphire speed.

R. F. S.

I find myself constantly praising the Creator for this colour!

"How little people know," adds C. S. Lewis, "*who think that holiness is dull. When one meets the real thing . . . it is irresistible.*" And I love it. It is His creation – like the kingfisher!

People of Jesus' day said all manner of things against Him, as He walked amongst them – *but no one ever said that He was dull*! They said, "No man spake like this Man!" It was the Pharisees and other religious leaders who by contrast were dull, droning out their prayers, standing in the marketplace, multiplying pettifogging laws and regulations, to lay a heavy weight upon men's spirits. Jesus, God's Son, was not like that. Had we no other evidence, the fact that little children were happy in His presence would be proof enough. "Take your religion," someone said, "and present it to a child. If it frightens him, and freezes the smile on his lips, whatever sort of religion it is, it is not Christianity. It lacks the essential light and colour of Jesus Christ." He set a little child in the midst of a group; He saw children at their games in the marketplace. His first public engagement was a wedding feast. Is it likely that a young couple and their parents would seek out a *dull* prophet to grace that occasion?

And the Good News that He proclaimed, we proclaim! It is a tragedy to neglect it, and a crime to make it dull.

What is the matter with us – or at least some of us? In a World Council of Churches' report broadcast from an Assembly, space was made to remind us *Christians* that "*the real dangers are complacency, lack of imagination,*

33

and the dull sense of hopelessness that settles upon those of little faith". It's distressing to find a great world gathering of Christian leaders feeling it necessary to say that to us who, in this age, follow Jesus Christ. *He was such a colourful character*. Speaking of His personality and His teaching, as revealed in the gospels now available in our language, Dorothy Sayers exclaims passionately: "If this is dull, then what, in heaven's name, is worthy to be called exciting? The people who hanged Christ never, to do them justice, accused Him of being a bore — on the contrary, they thought Him *too dynamic* to be safe."

If we allow our Christianity to lose its "colour", it will limp where it ought to dance. It is the easiest thing in the world, says Dr F. Townley Lord, "*to tone down the message of Jesus until it is almost colourless!* Almost insensibly, for example, we have toned down His teaching about sin and judgement. (This is understood as a reaction from the crudities and exaggerations of the Christian teaching of years ago.) But none need fear the strong words of Jesus about sin, for they are matched by words of unutterable grace and beauty about sinners."

I cling to what Florence Allshorn – founder of St Julian's House of refreshment, in the English countryside – said for all time: "I hate being ineffective when it's leaders that the world is wanting. I *hate, hate, hate* being ordinary, and just nice, *but dull!*" (For myself, I can't think of any modern-day disciple of Christ who better underlined the damage that dullness does. She was herself always so beautifully alive, so responsive.)

If only we could all be like her, what an impact the Church could make – if only we could all pray: "*From dullness, good Lord, deliver us!*"

Saints Are All Around Us!

As I open wide the windows of my study each morning, I see before me, over trees and rooftops, the tall tower of the church where I worship. Forthwith, I pray for our minister, and for all sinners, and "saints without haloes" who find their way there.

Our church, unlike many I know, does not bear the name of a saint, bestowed at the time of its building and dedication; but I have from time to time been called to many others that do, to lead worship or to speak at some weekday gathering, and I always count that a privilege. One such church, but a short walk from my home, is "St George's", the Presbyterian church; about as far off in another direction is "St Peter's", the local Anglican church; and equally handy is "St Joseph's", the Catholic church. A little further off – over the Harbour Bridge – is "St John's" Methodist church; nearby is "St James's", Beresford Street; no great distance off, amid trees, stands "St Barnabas'" Anglican church in Mount Eden Road; a little further out of the city on the other side are "St Stephen's" chapel and "St Mary's" cathedral, both Anglican; and off a little further, "St Luke's" Presbyterian, and "St Hilda's" Anglican. And there are still other churches, where I have never so far been called to speak, including "St Matthew's", right in the heart of the city, and "St Patrick's" cathedral, a close neighbour.

So, I have reminders of saints everywhere in the names of these churches. Long before there were any church buildings anywhere in the world, there were, of course, "saints in Caesar's household", as we know on the New Testament authority of St Paul. And can anyone think of a more difficult setting? Other names borne by that impassioned character, Caesar, were Nero Claudius. In efforts to satisfy his secret physical desires, and to wreak vengeance on those who opposed him, he stopped at nothing. Our secular record covering the history of the time shocks us with the infamy associated with his name. He murdered his brother Octavius, *and his own mother*. And in time – after a short reign of but fourteen inglorious years – being himself then only thirty years of age, he committed suicide in order to escape death at the hands of his own soldiers. Terrible!

Despite all this, there were "saints in Caesar's household"! Paul passed on words of sterling encouragement from those men and women of magnificent spirit. To mutual followers of their Lord in Philippi, he wrote: "All the saints salute you, chiefly they that are of Caesar's household" (Philippians 4:22).

A "saint" in the New Testament sense was never "a perfect character", but rather *a forgiven sinner*. The word used for a character, or a thing, perfectly whole, was *hieros*; but the word the New Testament translates as "saint" is *hagios* – that is, a thing or person, irrespective of any past history, *now wholly offered to God*. This was the true meaning of sainthood. It was to such people that Paul addressed greetings in lots of places besides "Caesar's household", for they were soon widely scattered. They must sometimes have been lonely, for of course they had no New Testament to help them, as we have – not to mention the other Christian literature now available. The truth is, they dared, women as courageously as men, to belong to "an underground movement", cost what it might. And in many cases it cost them the misery of the gibbet (a form of gallows); or subjection to the thumbscrew, or to suffering and death by burning faggots. (Today, Amnesty International informs us, men and women in some parts of the world are still imprisoned for their faith, and persecuted in cruel ways.)

So the centuries are strangely linked with those to whom Paul wrote: "Unto the church of God which is at Corinth . . . called to be saints" (1 Corinthians 1:2); "To the saints and faithful brethren in Christ which are at Colosse" (Colossians 1:2). Professor Herbert Butterfield, a vital historian at Cambridge in our day, wrote in his widely read *Christianity and History*: "It is impossible to measure the vast difference that ordinary Christian piety has made to the last two thousand years of European history." And he went on to underline it as *"the most moving spectacle that history affords"*.

We have to thank God that He still goes on making saints in the most real way. *These are still, we find, ordinary men and women – made extraordinary – wholly devoted to God*. So we look to our New Testament, rather than to our Oxford Dictionary, for a definition, because the latter only says: "A saint is a person canonized or officially recognized by the Church, as having won by exceptional holiness, a high place in heaven, and veneration on earth."

Oh, no! There have long been "saints without haloes". Some people, it seems, find it as hard to define a saint as others do to define a Christian. Someone once asked Josiah Royce, sitting in his study at Harvard University (as I learned lately when I was there), "What is your definition of a Christian?" That great philosopher had to say, "I don't know how to define a Christian." Then lifting his eyes to look out of his study window, he as quickly added, "But wait! There goes Phillips Brooks!" And that was his answer in terms of life – a definition on two legs, *a warm, loving, serving person not to be understood apart from Christ*. Not perfect – but whatever his past, in time wholly dedicated to God.

The very remembrance of such characters blesses us, so loving are such lives, so timeless, so down to earth!

One person of earlier times challenges me, whom you

may not even have heard of. She has, I discovered to my surprise, a statue in Westminster Abbey, along with kings and queens, the good and the great. She is *Saint Uncumber*! Of royal Portuguese descent, her special service was in relieving women of burdensome obligations. The word "cumber", of course, is in our dictionary – meaning "to hamper, hinder, burden" – but it isn't on our tongue often these days, although we know only too well what it means in day-to-day living. We used to talk about "weeds cumbering the ground", and "sin cumbering the earth". Today, we manage somehow to convey the same bothersome reality in other words. But it is still as real, unfortunately.

In the New Testament we come across the word in that lovely setting of Bethany. Some of us have chosen to recall it by walking the mile or so out over the hill from Jerusalem, to the loved setting of hospitality which was the little home of Martha, Mary and Lazarus. Our Lord valued that ever open door, and went there often. But there is no forgetting the unhappy word picture that Luke gives us in chapter ten. Things went awry that day, and we know why: Martha was "fussed". Luke's words are unforgettable (Luke 10:38–40): "Now it came to pass, as they went, that He entered into a certain village: and a certain woman named Martha received Him into her house. And she had a sister called Mary, which also sat at Jesus' feet, and heard His word. *But Martha was cumbered about much serving.*" Poor Martha! Poor everybody! – it was an off-day. "And Jesus answered and said unto her, Martha, Martha, thou art careful and troubled about many things: but one thing is needful." (What a pity she had allowed her beautiful gift of hospitality to fall out of focus, its one clear, loving line to be so spoilt!) The New English Bible says: "Martha was distracted by her many tasks . . ." We hardly need that modern translation – we know only too well what being "cumbered" means. It surprises us – be-

cause her dilemma is one so widespread – though Luke is
the only gospel scribe who makes room for this sad word
picture of frustration. It reads as if our Lord had never
seen Martha in that kind of dither before, and we can only
hope that His coming over their doorstep never
occasioned that unhappy mood again. For it spoilt things,
spoilt them utterly; so much so, that our Lord had to deal
with His hostess firmly. "Martha, Martha," He had to say
to her (as our New English Bible translates His words),
"you are fretting and fussing about so many things . . !"

And they were good things – but things that got in the
way of her giving *herself*, pushing out of perspective a
joyous welcome, fellowship, a readiness to listen, spiritual
realities. Is He saying that a man on a journey, however
hungry, has need of more than variously prepared food
for his body – good as that is – because he is more than
body?

Sometimes our deeply established pride in doing things
well trips us up – we are *cumbered* with much serving; we
fuss to keep up our reputation. Pots and pans, or agendas
for meetings, mean so much to us. They are, of course,
important – but some of us need to develop more deeply
the secret skills of Saint Uncumber.

Perhaps a little prayer I came upon lately can help:

> 'Mid all the traffic of the ways,
> Turmoils without, within,
> Make in my heart a quiet place,
> And come and dwell therein.
>   Anon

Surprises Keep Coming!

Have you had any surprises lately – at home, at your place of work, in your church?

Of course, I must add "the church" – for they come to us there, mainly, in fresh truths revealed; but in other ways, too.

On my very first night, in the very first church to which I was sent after training, the people gathered to give me what they called "A Welcome" – under the leadership of a steward, a layman.

"Well," he began, "we're very glad you've come. We thought we would have had a man! But, I suppose, if we can't have a whole loaf, we can make the best we can of *half a loaf!*" (I must say, I was as surprised as any; but secretly, in that moment, I determined that, by the grace of God, in no way would I ever be "*half* a loaf"!) Nobody today would address a woman that way, I hope.

Travel in those days, in that widely scattered mountain country, with unsealed roads and inadequate transport, was very strenuous, not only for me but for very many of the people whom I served. It was there that I ventured forth on the first of my two old motor-cycles.

At the end of two pioneer country charges – each with a clutch of widely scattered preaching places – when an economic depression managed to get our entire country in its grip, I was called north to the Methodist Social Service Mission in the country's largest city.

Those years were full of surprises – some very humanly amusing, some tragic, amongst courageous and out-of-work people, with a number of them already involved in the city's prisons and courts. Many with health and

40

strength were helped to go into the country in search of work; but nobody could gain entry into a "Work Camp" without a sound pair of boots. (And many an early morning I spent bending over a last – as my father taught me to do – half-soling boots given us by sympathetic folk who constantly sorted out their old clothes and boots for us.) In fact, nothing in those desperate days was counted amiss. Sacks of vegetables; old spectacles by the score; even long-finished-with false teeth, that I could sell in the city for the gold pins that could be extracted from them. A helpful second-hand dealer, with a cluttered shop on a nearby corner, brought me all sorts of things: children's prams and push-carts with one or two wheels missing; football cases without any bladders; bicycle wheels, but no frames. I refused nothing. One day, one of my bunch of helpers answered a knock at the Mission door to receive a perfectly good tombstone. What its history was, or where it came from, I never learned. It was one of the flat sort, with a substantial base of stone to stand on. To the surprise of all of us, it bore no name, only the words "Here lies the body of a British hero. Amen". Amongst our faithful helpers was a wit (and I can't think how we would have managed without him, on many occasions when there were heavy boxes to lift; or when we were at a loss either to find shelf and drawer room for what came in, or to know where to get more stuff. How tired we got in that Old Clothes Room!) I remember that morning, when to our surprise the tombstone arrived, that I happened to be wrestling with a bothersome oncoming cold. And our wit, pausing a moment at his work, called us all to hear a suggestion: "I think we shouldn't put this in the Jumble Sale just yet, but hang on to it for a bit – let's first see how Sister's cold turns out. After all, we could easily put 'INE' on the end of 'HERO'."

Happily, they never did; I sold that surprising possession to an old pensioner myself for five shillings – in two instalments. And she came with a child's push-cart, and carried it away, also in two instalments. Where she came from, or where she took it, I've no idea.

A little later, I put on my coat and went home. I tried first my usual smart walk in the good sweet air, but this time it did nothing for me. Not at all sure what the trouble was, my home-sharing friend, Rene, rang the doctor.

His first question was, "Where have you been?" And the story of the Old Clothes Room, as part of my Social Service work, came out. To give him a balanced idea, I went on: "Of course, that's not all. I share in leading Worship; and I run an 'Adventure Group' for young folk; superintend a Sunday School; and have duties at the Prison, and the Courts; and I run a Study group, and interview many dozens of people every week, as a kindly listening ear, when they need to pour out their anxieties. And I speak to a weekly Women's Meeting; and organize a weekly Sewing Guild; and gather up a Sunday morning children's choir, and motor out for the choir-master to a distant suburb; and daily check the records of all who call, in the hope that we can give them some kind of material help, or get a spindly child into the Mission Health Camp. Till the Depression, many of these had never had need to apply for any kind of family help, and were shy about going on a city list. But this, we have discovered, is essential", I added, "to make the money and goods spread fairly. It's a lot of listening and note-taking, and visiting people in their homes all over the city. And checking out the too-eager ones, and the sick and aged, unable to come on their own account."

"But let us get back to the Old Clothes Room", said my quietly listening doctor. Then he drew Rene aside, for talk in the passage. "How are you situated?" was his next question. "Can you nurse her? I have to tell you", said he, returning to my bedside, "that you have a germ on the lining of your heart – the kind of germ likely to be lodging in grubby old clothes. So stay where you are – quite flat, no pillow, no moving about, and I'll come again tomorrow!"

To Rene, going out to the front door, he said, "I'm afraid it's going to be a long job. Perhaps we should send her to hospital. I wonder if you'll be able to manage, with all you've got to do. Think it over – I'll come again tomorrow."

He came, as arranged, on the morrow, and on the morrow, and on many months of morrows! From time to time an additional medical opinion was brought in, each saying much the same, but one adding: "Well, it's stiff at your age. I think you'll have to accept the possibility that you'll never work again." Another said, "Never walk again" – perhaps he meant up-hill. Nobody seemed to suggest any other treatment than what my doctor was giving me; but nothing more was said about my going to hospital. Mention was made once or twice of the helpful quietness of my room. And the months went on. Every day I could be sure of seeing my doctor. So concerned, so faithful he was! And Rene came in and regularly she changed all my pictures!

And months passed before I was able to rise from my bed each day, leaving my pile of books behind. Rene borrowed them from friends, and brought them from the Library, to help the time go by, when she was taken up with her music teaching, housekeeping, and secretarial responsibilities of the Presbyterian Youth Movement that she served, throughout the land. I could do little to help whilst still in bed – save pod the peas for dinner, when they were in season, or other such modest jobs as preparing the strawberries she brought in from the garden. But at least, she knew how things were going, and the doctor came every morning.

As a friend, she was doing wonderful things to help me. She knew that my money had all but run out, but she saw no problem in that so long as she was earning. "A day may come", she said, "when there is a change in events – and you can help me then!" And that day did come eventually.

I don't remember now who suggested that a long sea-trip might be beneficial, when I'd been getting about on level places with a stick. My mother came up from the South Island, on a brief visit. I don't know what she thought of the figure before her – a ghost of myself. That was her surprise. I learned to pray at a deeper level, seeking the Will of God. I never doubted but that He had work for me to do; but just then, I couldn't tell what it would be. It was Rene who suggested *it might be writing*. Nobody dreamed that I would still be writing over fifty-two years later, when her life here came to an end, paying her a Tribute in the closing pages of my latest book, fittingly titled. "CONTINUALLY AWARE!"

* * *

But you and I shouldn't be surprised. There are surprises all the way through the Cristian life, and especially notable are those associated with our Lord's Death and Resurrection.

Two men with whom He joined – heads down and sad, on the way home to Emmaus – spoke their grief, adding, "Our own hopes were that He would be the redeemer of Israel – but He is dead, and that is three days ago!" However there was no forgetting their next statement, on which their whole world changed: *"Though some women of our number gave us a surprise*; they were at the Tomb, early in the morning and could not find His body, but they came to tell us they had actually seen a vision of angels who declared *He was alive"* (Luke 24:22; Moffatt). *What a "surprise"! And in the place of Death!* (Our Risen Lord's own words are recorded for us in the gospel (John 14:19; A.V.): *"Because I live, ye shall live also!"*)

Surprises Keep Coming!

It is not a great deal to say on so great an issue, but coming from Him, it is enough for peace of mind. "If Christ be not risen", says a passage in 1 Corinthians 15:14; A.V., "then is our preaching vain, and your faith is also vain." But we have every certainty that He is risen! And Life awaits us after Death! What it will be like, we do not know – that waits for us as "a surprise". "At this stage in my Christian experience", said the beloved Archbishop William Temple, "there is nothing in the world of which I feel more certain. *I have no idea what it will be like*, and I am glad that I have not!"

Newness of Life

Very early this morning, I set out to catch the post. As I turned my corner into the quite imposing street comprising places of business, I saw the little florist's shop, lately moved to its new position a few doors up. And there, beyond spacious windows, were bowls of golden daffodils, the first of the season!

The next minute a printed scroll, delightfully designed, engaged my attention. It read: "PUT A LITTLE SPRING INTO SOMEONE'S LIFE!" It was a sales notion, I knew, but in an instant it was saying more to me than that – much more. Apart from buying a Spring bunch to carry to someone shut in, sick or sad, I realized that in eagerly tending my own little patch of front garden from which I had just set out, I was putting a little Spring into someone's life! For it astonished me again and again that passers-by stopped to say as much, when they have chanced on me there wrestling with weeds.

Later this morning the postman brought me, among others, a letter from a friend in the country, a day's travel away. Spring had found her, too, adding to daffodils "weeping willows down by the stream, all out in their tender leafage. Everywhere, new buds were breaking into colour; birds practising their newest songs". It was good to be alive.

Spring in our country doesn't come with quite the "sudden glorious shock" that it does in England – but for all that, it is a miracle. On my first Spring in England, I shouldered a haversack and, with a friend, tramped down into Kent, along the "Pilgrims' Way". With orchards and gardens awakening, we noticed it was the sixteenth day of

April – or, as more poetic writers would earlier have put it, "XVI daye of Aprylle". (When I got back I wrote a book in praise of it, which I entitled *When We Two Walked* – now out of print, though I still get requests for it.) And each time the season comes round, I find myself praying that my earthly life will not run out before I am able to share once more in the miracle of an English Spring.

* * *

I know that I have been fortunate. Among Spring memories, added to those that made my first English Spring so memorable, was a later stay in Lilian Cox's charming cottage, on the fringe of Chale Green on the Isle of Wight. It was early enough to find icicles still tapering from the window ledges each morning, but sunshine blessed each day.

Yet another English Spring, I was privileged to spend days and nights in the old Quaker hostel of "Jordans", amid Buckinghamshire's glorious beech woods.

And in between, English friends have addressed lyrical letters to me, eagerly at work on the other side of the world. One of these friends – knowing my joy in the English Spring – kindly copied out for me a poem she had written and published, called "The Apple Tree":

> to know that such an ancient tree,
> Inlaid with lichen, bent with years,
> Will bear, *each Spring*, such tender buds,
> Is talisman against my fears.
>
> For pink and white against the grey,
> The certain innocence renewed,
> Comforts the heart convincingly
> Before the next dark interlude.
>
> Muriel Grainger

One early morning in Cambridge, my colour camera slung over my shoulder, I walked beyond college lawns and old mellow walls to Rupert Brooke's "Grantchester". Tall, over-arching trees blessed me; and I passed the old house where once he lived. I found myself mulling over some of his poems that had accompanied my growing up, and which that day seemed as fresh as ever. I could not help but wonder what more he might have written, had not war broken in upon his brief adventure. Pausing awhile before the tall memorial cross inscribed with the young poet's name among others, I found no answer. But I was glad to find on that Spring morning, circling its base, a ring of freshly opened crocuses. For hope is an essential spirit of every Spring.

* * *

"Never lose an opportunity to see something beautiful", Charles Kingsley had said to his son, a young Englishman, long before ever Rupert Brooke passed along this earthly way. "Beauty", he rejoiced to add, "is God's handwriting." And surely it is. He has so much to say to us, all our life long – and especially, it seems, Spring by Spring.

I had this underlined for me one season in my own country, when I returned home from travelling afar in the service of my church, ministering beside its President for a year. In the course of considerable speaking and writing, I came to tree-blessed, garden-blessed Nelson, where I had grown up.

Many times I had driven into the little city by way of Bishopdale, climbing slowly enough at that point, in the family horse and trap. Never before had I actually entered those open gates at the beginning of the winding way, but I came just then as guest of the Bishop and Mrs Hulme-Moir. And an unforgettable morning of fellowship it was! After tea and talk, a pile of books I had written was brought out for me to sign.

Spring was in the air, and there was no keeping it out of our conversation. Presently the Bishop's wife spoke of little Ian. "Many times", she began with a smile, "I've had reason to thank God for what I've learned from our children. Ian was very much mine, for his father went away to war when he was less than two, and did not come home until he was eight and a half. As a little fellow of three or four, he loved to listen to the morning devotions over the air. The sound of the organ would bring him running from his play, to sit cross-legged with his back against the radio cabinet. One morning", she went on, "dear old Archdeacon Begbie was speaking, with all the force of his great spirituality. Suddenly, the child burst into the kitchen where I was washing dishes; he had just caught one phrase, and was turning it over in his mind. 'Mummy, what's "newness of life"?' For a moment", she said, "I was stumped: how did one explain to a child of three or four, this profound miracle? Then my eyes lighted on some daffodil bulbs lying on the kitchen table, waiting to be planted. I gathered them up and, taking the child's hand, I said, 'Come, I'll show you. Do you see these bulbs? They're really beautiful flowers, but they don't look like that now, for God hasn't wakened them yet. We'll plant them in the garden, and then watch.'

"We went into the garden, found a little patch of soil, and planted the bulbs. Day after day, little Ian would run down the garden to look. Gradually the weeks passed, and Winter turned to Spring. Then one morning I was greeted with a wild shout: 'Mummy, Mummy, come and see! They're up!' And they were. A few afternoons later our local minister called, and as we walked and talked in the garden, he suddenly exclaimed, 'You've got a lovely patch of daffodils there.' Ian looked at him with fine scorn for a moment, then he said, 'They're not daffodils; they's newness of life! Didn't you know that, Mr Gabbot?'"

I begged Mrs Hulme-Moir's permission to re-tell that

Spring experience, not only because it was a reminder of the freshness and wonder of the child mind, but because it was centred in a miracle of lasting significance!

"Newness of life" is, of course, a New Testament phrase. Paul used it in a letter to his friends (Romans 6:4): "Like as Christ was raised up from the dead by the glory of the Father, even so *we also should walk in newness of life*." Paul is talking, not only of life after death (which would be a new and wonderful thing), but of life here, after a Christian's confession of faith in the Risen Christ. It is, at heart, the glory of our Christian experience – and every Springtime God gives us a reminder of it. As a commentator says in *The Interpreter's Bible*, "Our fellowship includes the moral adventure of living a new kind of life [with a new kind of beauty about it, and liveliness, and purpose]. The verb Paul uses is admirably chosen to make clear the nature of our understanding. To *walk* requires effort. It is also a means of proceeding from one point to another, and it presupposes that we have a goal before us . . . *We walk in newness of life*."

When it is Springtime in the heart, it is Springtime everywhere! "We live in the Springtime of spiritual things, because Jesus lived – and lives."

> *New* mercies each returning day
> Hover around us while we pray;
> *New* perils past, *new* sins forgiven,
> *New* thoughts of God, *new* hopes of heaven.
>   Keble

Now and Always

Was our hostess lonely, I wondered, or was she unusually devout? I don't know. But I'll never forget her request. Many miles out beyond his own country town high in the hills, my country carpenter friend and I set off to visit a still more distant homestead. At one stage, as we climbed up and down in his old lorry, I thought we'd never get there, but as the Summer afternoon drew in we came to a typical New Zealand gate. I accepted the hint to get down and open it and, what was as important, close it again after we had passed through. Beyond the gracious homestead that now came into view, there were many cattle. Our host and hostess, who had been watching for us for an hour or so, came out to welcome us in. The kettle, we were assured, would be on the boil "in a twinkling". And that was good news, for we had come a great many hilly miles.

Soon, anyone looking in would have found it hard to believe that the four of us had never met until that moment. There was such friendliness over the tea.

Then, it happened: the men went off to do their business, and we two women continued with our admiration of the garden. Knowing that I was a trained churchwoman (having read several of my books), the kindly wife explained to me that they almost never got to church, save on those rare occasions when they chanced to be on holiday with relations. The distance was too great. Then she led me on, into a wonderful stand of trees, tall under the sky; and when I remarked on them, their beautiful boles reaching up like the pillars of a cathedral, she went on to confess: "Yes, this really is my cathedral. I am glad

51

you feel like that, too. I hoped you would, and that during your brief visit we might worship here together."

And we did! It was very simple – I don't now recall what words I used. Although I have led worship so often, this was a unique experience.

In a little book I've lately come upon, *Short Prayers for the Long Day* by Giles and Melville Harcourt (to which I contributed), is a beginner's prayer, written by Ellen Frances Gilbert, that brings to the forefront of my mind the worship experience of that late Summer afternoon. (We were *not beginners*, of course, either of us – far from it.) I now ask permission of our mutual publishers, Collins, to quote the poem of the one who wrote:

> Let me be quiet now, and kneel,
>   Who never knelt before,
> Here, where the leaves paint patterns light
>   On a leaf-strewn forest floor;
> For I, who saw no God at all
>   In sea or earth or air,
> Baptized by beauty, now look up
>   To see God everywhere.

It is gloriously possible to find God in Nature; but I am confident that will always be an emasculated faith, without what is revealed of Him within the scriptures of the Old and New Testaments, and the experience of church folk up through the centuries.

Jesus spent nights alone with God, up on the hills. He was a great Nature lover, but He never neglected to join with men and women in public worship. This reached back to childhood, and up through youth to manhood. Luke writes strikingly, in the early part of his gospel (4:16): "And He came to Nazareth, where He had been brought up: and, *as His custom was*, He went into the synagogue on the sabbath day."

(Doubtless many of His fellow worshippers were dull, but it made no difference. He paused to worship God, His eternal Father. Doubtless the actual building seemed to a young man a little shabby, but it made no difference. Maybe the old priest, whose business it was to lead worship, seemed dreary at times, but that was no obstacle.) The words of the Psalmist, written long before, echoed in that young man's heart: "Worship the Lord in the beauty of holiness!" In our day, although much has changed, the principles of worship remain the same. It is pleasant, of course, to assemble with others in a place conducive to worship (and our churches ought to be as helpful and as beautiful as we can make them), "*but nothing*", as Saint Benedict once said, "*must precede the worship of God.*"

"And what, at heart, in this twentieth century, is worship?" someone wanted to know, when I answered his question about what I was writing. To start with, I had to reply that it is, all the world around, surprisingly varied. *There is no one way*, as my friend, Dr Alan Brash, underlined in a conversation shared a while ago in my home. He was preparing a talk in the "Faith for Today" series, to be broadcast for mid-morning radio listeners; and later, after I had heard his talk, he kindly gave me his permission to quote from it.

"People who live by a deep trust in God," he began, "express that in an amazing variety of ways. Some of those ways can be quite embarrassing to an observer, especially when people show all the outward signs of great emotion as they express their worship. In Africa," he went on, "I worshipped with Christians who literally danced before God, and then prayed with their foreheads on the floor and their shoes removed from their feet. In a remote Indonesian island I visited a pastor who went about his jungle parish always barefooted, but when he had a specially solemn service of worship to conduct, he put on his only pair of shoes. In the Soviet Union I worshipped with a man, well over eighty years of age, who knelt in a position of total humility for nearly two hours. And there are other varieties.

"Unfortunately," my friend went on, "religious people have always had a pressing desire to achieve conformity in both doctrine and forms of worship. They have had an almost incurable tendency to deny the reality of other people's faith, if it was differently expressed from their own. But what a tragedy that is. Surely it is perfectly obvious that in every aspect of this creation, God has rejoiced *in infinite variety – not in uniformity*.

"Fortunately, at last many of us Christian people are, in our time, becoming aware that God receives, forgives and blesses all sorts of people, however different they are from each other. Thanks be, we have given up trying to shut one another out – or, most of us have.

"There are, of course, certain fruits which faith in God – in all its variety of expression – does demand of us, if it is to be called a Christian faith. First, there is the indestructible conviction (despite all the evidence of the power of evil, all the economic injustice, nuclear war preparations, and the rest) that the love of God is the ultimate power beyond all powers. Evil may crucify that love, but we know that His love out-suffers evil till evil disintegrates. That is the sure reality of the hope which faith creates, and which defeats despair . . .

"Second," he went on, "our faith, however expressed, must make each of us a channel of that same love in all human relationships. In our families, of course; also among the disadvantaged and the suffering in our wider community – the unemployed, the handicapped, the broken . . . Yes, and even those far away, like the oppressed black people in South Africa, or the hundred children abandoned each month in Rio de Janeiro . . . reaching out without limit. This, whatever its form of expression, is truly a faith for today, for it transforms life."

"Yes," I found myself adding, "I believe that!"

"Worship", to borrow the words of the beloved Archbishop William Temple, "*is the main business of the church.*" It was from the beginning, and always will be. To worship God is to make a proclamation about His nature, in terms of prayer and praise and exhortation. And it can happen, I am convinced, in a glade of great trees; as in a lowly building raised by men's hands; or in a glorious cathedral – indeed, wherever human hearts acknowledge Him in sincerity and truth.

My heart leapt when I came upon the simple, beautiful words of a fifth-century collect:

> Bless all who worship Thee,
> From the rising of the sun
> Unto the going down of the same.
> Of Thy goodness, give us;
> With Thy love, inspire us;
> *By Thy Spirit, guide us*;
> By Thy power, protect us;
> In Thy mercy, receive us,
> Now and always. Amen.

Our Travels

"Travel", most say, "broadens the mind." I often wonder. Sometimes, I think, it only "broadens the feet", as dear Professor Murdock suggested.

But we moderns all like to travel, over our own country from end to end, or overseas. Those who don't are few, and they charge the rest of us with suffering from *travelitis furiosis*. They say we are no sooner in one place than we are packing our bags again, off to some other place. It is true that many of us attempt too much – fifteen countries in fourteen days! It can be done, if one starts off by air. But what does it all add up to? A few strange or fascinating things, a few familiar ones.

I travelled by bus, once, away down from Sydney to Melbourne, and on to Adelaide. It doesn't look far on the map, but it's a great distance, as is the distance from my own country to Australia, even to begin the tour I have instanced – some thirteen hundred and forty-three miles by air!

On that long bus trip south, we made stops here and there, in towns and cities. In one of them, at the end of an hour, two smiling passengers came back to rejoin the bus. When someone remarked on their obvious pleasure, one of them said eagerly, "Oh yes, we had a lovely time – *we found Woolworths!*"

We each bring home something, but what would such travellers bring? Only a customs official, I suppose, could answer that. It is part of his responsibility to open bags, with his question: "What have you got to declare?" I have talked pleasantly with many a person at his work the world round, but never, I have to admit, with a customs official. Maybe that's a pity! He must have many good stories, hovering between amusement and amazement! But he cannot share them. He's not allowed to and there's no time for more than two civil questions, as his quick hands sift through the contents of each case: "Any cigarettes? Any spirits?" He dare not ask, *"Any experiences you'll treasure all your days?"* They are not on any customs list. Already, I note that he is trying to press down, as best he can, my once tidy packing, and marking the end of my closed case with a piece of chalk, before turning away with the oft-repeated word, "Next!"

I do not complain, of course. I'm *through* the customs!

He will never know that *the richest things I'm bringing home from overseas are memories.* And the very richest of them all one year, that of a lark soaring high over Assisi. There was no duty on that; or on the little poem I wrote of my visit. I titled it, "Harvest Days in Assisi". The great wains drawn by the white oxen were coming in, heaped high, as we lunched day by day on the edge of the farmyard. I wrote:

> Problems bruise my mind, but not here –
> in Saint Francis' setting, all is as golden
> as a slat of sunlight through the door,
> as simple as the creatures of God's giving.
>
> Up on the hill, church doors stand open,
> the people going with a canticle of praise,
> some from village homes in little streets,
> some from the far world with eyes of curiosity.
>
> Down here, near the kindly olives
> is the water trough, and at harvest
> those faithful to God's earthy purpose,
> raise the golden stacks and guide the white oxen.

Long, abrasive centuries make no difference,
God's lark rises, and His seasons turn,
cupped in the friendly contour of the hills,
these simple things of the heart live on.

                                        R. F. S.

Five days later I had to leave that setting of humble, holy things, and go down from that hill town to which Saint Francis brought renown.

Buildings raised there through all the centuries reminded us of his spirit; stone figures, paintings and frescoes from the early masters spelled out his love of God's humblest creatures. Such a place of pilgrimage, praise and prayer!

That early morning when I knew it first, the grasses lapped my ankles and, for my special joy it seemed, a lark rose vertically into the blue and hung just out of sight, his trembling song reaching down to me. A slender song, attributed to one such, came freshly to my memory:

> See where I live,
>   In deep grass,
> Where the little
>   Shadows pass.
>
> See where I sing,
>   In steep height,
> All amid
>   The glowing light.
>
> Hark! I have bound
>   Earth and sky
> Fast, with cords
>   Of minstrelsy.
>   Anon

We have on record Saint Francis' love for the larks of Assisi. "If I were to speak to the Emperor," said he, "I would, supplicating and persuading him, tell him for the love of God and me, to make a special law that no man should take or kill sister larks nor do them any harm."

Saint Francis' joy, expressed by the soaring larks, remained undiminished to the very end of his life and gentle ministry. Years before ever I was able to go to Assisi, I read Ernest Raymond's book, *In the Steps of St Francis*; and when the glad day came for me to pack my bag for Italy's great cities, and little Assisi, I took care to put it in. As I lunched day by day with two close friends, under the shady olives, we shared the experience of reading aloud. And it all became real in our hearts: we were looking at what he looked at, and rejoicing in what he rejoiced in. *From the grass that welcomed us, the larks went up – and their message was one of joy!*

I remember when together we read of Francis' death, surrounded by his serving brothers. To quote Ernest Raymond: "They watched with him all that night; and the first light of Friday the second of October began to come . . . But Francis could distinguish light from darkness no more, and thinking it was still Thursday, he said, 'I should like you to bring me a loaf which we will break and eat together as our Master did the Thursday before He died.'

"'But this is not Thursday,' they told him gently, 'it is Friday now.'

"'I thought it was still Thursday.'

"Still, the loaf was brought, and he broke it for them, and each ate his fragment, a symbol of his share in their common love.

"'Now read to me the Gospel for Maundy Thursday', said Francis. They fetched the book and read that Gospel for the Thursday before Easter.

"All that day they saw him slowly sinking, but just as

the sun of Saturday, 3rd October 1226, was dropping
down towards the mountains . . . and as all noticed with
joy, *the larks were singing loudly in the last of the day*,
Francis was heard to sing, too . . . Soon the watching
brothers saw that he was dead. And they wrote afterwards
of the peace and happiness in his face. They wrote also
that 'in the silence they heard the larks singing'."

* * *

"*What joy there must be in the heart of God*," added James
Gilmour, a later Christian, "*to keep so many larks in
ecstasy!*"

The Joy of Recognition

Joy that meets us in this generous life is of so many kinds;
but among the most valued, to me, is *the joy of recognition*.

The very first day I stepped into London, my ears and
eyes alert, I heard clearly an old childhood jingle:

> "Oranges and lemons",
>   Say the bells of St Clement's.
> "You owe me five farthings",
>   Say the bells of St Martin's.
> "And when will you pay me?"
>   Say the bells of Old Bailey.

In a space nearby that day was the old church of St
Clement Danes, its bells ringing out. In an early history
book I'd happened on long before, I'd read how the
Danes had come up the river into London and settled.

Now, once a year, it seemed, the children of St
Clement's welcomed little poor children to their old
church, decorated for this special day with boughs of
oranges and boughs of lemons, as I was to see, to my
delight.

When everybody had crowded in, we had a service.
And later (the doors re-opened and the bells still ringing),
each child was given in one hand an orange, and in the
other a lemon. I'll never forget it, that first experience of
London, centred on *the joy of recognition*.

* * *

Today, the postman brought me a fine letter from Shona Caughey, a fellow traveller, from the far side of our city, underlining this joy. And she gave me permission to quote her. "During the Second World War," she began, "my husband was billeted with a family in a small Italian village. Recently we returned to that village, now a sizeable town. All we had to help us look for the family were my husband's hazy memories and a small black and white snapshot of two pretty girls aged seventeen and eighteen, Elia and Elisa – a photograph taken thirty-seven years before.

"We arrived in Ceretto d'Esi in the late afternoon. We walked round what had been the old village centre. Now and then, when we met an elderly person, we showed our photo, hoping for some sign of recognition. No, sadly, with a shake of the head, it meant nothing.

"We stayed in a small hotel for the night, and next morning were resigned to travelling on without finding those we sought. It was Sunday, and I walked over into the old church in the square. I always feel a little diffident about asking what could be called self-centred requests of the Almighty, but I did pray that morning that we might find Elia and Elisa.

"When we were ready to travel on, north-east to Ancona, we decided to have a last look around the square. An old lady was watching us from a corner window. I reached up with the photo to show her, and with a few stumbling words in Italian, conveyed our problem. She disappeared with our photo, and for a moment I was anxious; but she came back with her spectacles and stared hard at the snapshot. Then, 'Si, si!' she said. She came through the door and indicated that we should follow her. In a manner recognizable in any language, she apologized for her curlers, her old dress and her slippers.

"She led us down several little streets, and up a flight of steps – it must have been about a kilometre – before she stopped at a neat two-storeyed cottage, and rang the bell. Two white heads appeared at the top window, and she pointed to my husband, Bill, with a rapid explanation.

"Their faces were transformed. 'Beel! Beel!' they called together in great excitement, and came down quickly to let us in.

"Our helpful old lady went home then, with a tactful excuse of something that had to be done, and we joined Elia and Elisa in their small, attractive sitting room. I couldn't understand any of their excited chatter, though my husband followed enough to contribute an odd word in Italian. *But the joy of recognition was overwhelming!*

"Their mother had been kind to the young soldier pushed into their home.

"'Madre?' Bill asked.

"'Morte', they said, for a moment subdued . . .

"They had lived in Rome for about twenty years, and had only recently returned to the old house.

"To me", Shona summed up, "they were complete strangers, and we couldn't communicate at all. But we experienced a joy that transformed our physical barriers."

* * *

This, to me, was also the secret of one of my most loved incidents in the New Testament. John builds up the word picture, in John 20:1–18. His Lord had been brutally captured under the shadows of Gethsemane's trees, where He had gone, by night, to pray; He had been led away, unjustly judged, lashed, and after staggering out beyond the city wall to a high place, crucified between earth and heaven on a Roman cross.

But that, of course, was not all, as Dr William Barclay reminded us when he recounted the story of Mary's early morning experience at the tomb, entitling it "The Great Recognition", and he could nowhere have found a more telling title for that glorious experience on the world's first Easter morning!

Jesus had conquered death. He had risen, and *had called Mary by her own name* as she stood there tearfully, with no use now for her burial spices. She had seen in a moment that He was not the gardener, and had joyously responded, "Rabboni!" – "Master!"

* * *

And did others known to us have experiences of their own? My poet friend Asa Johnson thinks so. In a poem he sent me, he says:

> It must have happened in the later years
> That Peter,
> Mary,
> Thomas,
> (Those who had been His friends)
> Would walk along the road where they had
>   been with Him,
> And say to their companions,
> "This is where He healed the lepers –
> There were ten, you know,
> And only one came back to thank Him.
> We were standing there beside that tree."
> Or, "This is where He took the children
> In His arms
> And blessed them.
> He was sitting on that rock."
>
> Familiar places must have held
> Such memories of Him,
> Almost as though He still were there
> And they could hear His voice.

So memories persist,
And we recall our meeting with the Master,
"I was here
When first I felt His living presence,
Knew within my deepest heart
He was my Saviour, too."
Or, "There His healing came to me",
Or, "Yonder is the place where first
My prayer became companionship with Him."

There is nothing quite like the joy of recognition!

Happy Families

Once upon a time, as it got dark outside, and we were snugly shut in at home, we used to play a card game called "Happy Families". Did you do that? Whether it's played nowadays, I don't know.

But I do know that there's no way of sharing an experience of "happy families" in our grown-up world, without observing a handful of rules. At first they might seem a little dull, but they're not, once you get going; for without them there would be no game. About us are many people who seem not to have grasped this: they just expect to take what they want, and when they want it. But that doesn't work – either in a game on Winter nights, or in real life. Experiences that ignore this fact are often very costly, and daily police court reports in the newspapers ought to be proof enough of that.

From the start God saw how it must be, if the game of "happy families" was to go on; as, in his turn, did the Psalmist, who said: *"God setteth the solitary in families"* (Psalm 68:6). And He has never given up an eager involvement in this whole matter. So Charter Piggott's little poem bears no date:

> Two lovers met
> In plighted troth,
> The secret woodland
> Hid them both,
> But God was at the meeting.

Of course! The setting up of families is of much importance to Him, as it is to each one of us from our earliest days: a babe, tender and dependent, with no language but a coo and a cry; soon, a small child, coming indoors with a bloodied knee from a fall on a hard path, or a black eye to comfort; or a little girl needing someone to show her how to thread a needle. Then come the questions that perplex: "What does God do when it gets dark?" and "How does He make wonderful things like mountains, and stars? And babies to match people?"

Well, yes, questions start early; and there always will be questions. Some we can puzzle out for ourselves, one by one, but it's good to face others in families. There will be lessons not only for *heads*, but for *hearts* as well. Boys and girls, and big people too, are not like favourite animals; they have inner spirits that know hunger, not merely for breakfast porridge or sugar-coated cookies, or other kinds of food, but for beautiful things, and heroes full of courage. Also there is a need of good people to follow (who fortunately can be parents). That's one of the really important reasons why "God setteth the solitary in families". Believe me, He likes playing "Happy Families" too!

I can never now thank Him enough for my experience of growing up. And I was delighted to hear Dr John Foster speak in the same strain, when I was on one of my early visits to England. He put it so well: "What a start I had – in a home where there was much laughter, and no fear; where forgiveness was always at hand; where one entered upon life as something wholesome and clean, with a standard set and a duty to be done. Religion was not terrifically talked about. It was everywhere assumed. I grew up knowing that it lay at the back of everything good in my inheritance. When I learned to say, 'Our Father', I knew what it meant."

It is a God-given gift. We are born to belong!

But this does not mean that we should wrap ourselves around with family pride – not at all. Sometimes family pride can actually be an unhappy thing. I remember the Pendyces. Their creed was shown us in a book we all read at one time, *The Country House*: "I believe in my father and in his father and in his father's father, the makers and keepers of our estate; and I believe in myself and my son and my son's son. And I believe that we have made the country and shall keep the country what it is. I believe in the public school, and especially the public school that I was at. And I believe in my social equals and the country house, and things as they are, for ever and ever. Amen."

This, of course, is not the sin solely of an English family where portraits painted through the years hang on the walls, and prideful traditions are handed down. But wherever it occurs, family pride of this sort is a sheer loss. Perhaps there are not many families like the Pendyces these days, even in England; the changing pattern of the times has seen to that.

But in families great and small – families like ours – it is still possible to know a lovely kind of "family pride". And we need it very much, in our community life. The simple truth is that light dies out of our eyes when we have no sense of "belonging". In God's plan, from the beginning, we were intended to belong. The loosening of marriage ties and the increase in divorce, added to the general rootlessness of our labouring conditions in many cases, make for joylessness. There is often a thinness, a brittleness, a lostness in our relationships. In the most worthwhile sense, it is impossible to be a complete person without other persons. God saw this need of ours, right from the very start. He said, "It is not good for man to live alone." And that is still true! It doesn't always mean marriage, of course, when one is old enough to move out into the world. Every child deserves a happy experience of family life, whatever his colour or clime. Happiness is not an extra, though it requires a sustained sense of interested pliability.

In his autobiography, *A Poet in the Family*, Dannie Abse writes with humour of the day he and his young son set off together to see a one-act play he had written. (But I must pass it on in his own direct speech.)

"'I think you'll like it', I said. 'It's rather funny as a matter of fact.'

"Off we went . . . On the way back I asked my small son, who seemed quite cheerful, what he thought of 'The Eccentric'. He cleared his throat. He hesitated. He turned his head toward me, serious, big-eyed, and pronounced, 'Only one thing wrong with it, Dad.'

"'What's that?'

"'It's boring', he said.

"A few days later, though, he came into the living room with Josh, one of his friends, and as I looked up from my newspaper, he pointed to one of the books I had written that, for some reason, happened to be lying on top of the bookcase.

"'See that thick book there, Josh?' he said.

"Pleased, I pretended to read the newspaper.

"'What?'

"'That book. That book on the top of the bookcase.'

"'Yes.'

"'Well,' continued David, proudly, '*my mother typed all of that.*'"

You see what I mean. *We mustn't take ourselves too seriously, in this serious game of "Happy Families".*

And, of course, it reaches up to God, who first thought it all out and set us upon our way. And is with us still! The truth is, the experience of belonging goes a great deal deeper down into the roots of being than a casual acknowledgement of things spiritual, and an occasional attendance at worship. It's not something that, entered upon, makes a little difference to a few things: it's something that, all the way, makes *all the difference to everything.*

Circumstances have an uncanny way of driving us back to essentials. Foremost is our need really to belong, if "Happy Families" is to be worth playing to the end. Psychiatrists are still telling us this, out of their experience of being called to patch things up. So are modern hospital chaplains and physicians, as well as ministers who, in visiting, often get very close to human needs such as this. The world takes on a fresh face when it is known to be God's world. The beauty of it becomes more beautiful when, in more than sparrows and mountains and skies, it expresses His care. The terrifying importance of human choice, as well as that of electricity, of atomic energy, and the partially understood mysteries of outer space, have to be thought of as part of God's Creation.

Dr H. H. Farmer, in our day, forsook for a time his theological phraseology to make this plain to us. "It is not", he felt moved to say to us, "that God creates a man, and then pops him into a world of persons, as a housewife makes a dumpling and pops it into the saucepan, both dumpling and saucepan being capable of existing apart from one another. To come into existence as a man," he sums up, "is to be incorporated in this world of the personal, *to be in relation to persons – the Divine and human persons – and existence is not possible on any other terms.*"

"And not desirable", do you want to add?

Belonging – from the very beginning, as I understand God's purpose, this was set to be its central wonder! And still is! Lately, Ailsa Miller, a nurse in our little country, wrote a poem on this, and kindly gave me permission to share it:

> Did God make
> The tree for the bird,
> Or the bird for the tree?

Happy Families

The sky for the clouds,
Or the clouds for the sky?

The earth for man,
Or man for the earth?

The sea for the fish,
Or the fish for the sea?

This I know –
*He made me for Himself,
And Himself for me.*

Heartfelt Thanks!

It would be a tremendous loss in this life to have no one to whom one could give thanks. I can't imagine it. Though Katherine Mansfield, our little country's famed storyteller, found herself in that dilemma. She was in Switzerland at the time, seeking health high up in the mountains. Her days were full of sunshine and tonic air, amid pine forests. But she found herself setting down words that have never been forgotten: "If only one could make some small, grasshoppery sound of praise to someone – thanks to someone – but who?"

The Psalmist, centuries before, had no such problem, and his words still dance up and down in our world: "Make a joyful noise unto the Lord . . . Know ye that the Lord, He is God . . . Enter into His gates with thanksgiving . . . *be thankful unto Him, and bless His name*. For the Lord is good, His mercy is everlasting; and His truth endureth to all generations" (Psalm 100: 4; A.V.).

It is wonderful to waken with thanks upon one's lips, with renewed energies, and work to do; with the fertility and beauty of the earth, and food for one's body. Even more precious is the fellowship of kindred spirits, in one's home and place of work, in one's neighbourhood and at the end of this great earth.

When dark days come, with serious decisions pressing, it is a supportive experience to know on one's shoulder the steadying arm of someone loved and trusted. And there are others who enrich through books, biographies and autobiographies especially. Many, sharing our world, would never be known to us otherwise.

I think of James Agate, only unofficially a religious

man, who five days before his death at sixty-five wrote: "I thank Thee, God, for all the things life has meant to me. For the seaside and cricket on the sands which made up my childhood. For the golf courses and show yards of my youth and middle age. For the books, acting and music, recollections of which make my old age rich and enviable. For the stone walls of Derbyshire, the dales of Yorkshire, Welsh mountains, and English lakes. For fun, good talk, and enjoyment of the mind of others. For brother Edward's wit and courage. For brother Harry, who has taught me what unselfishness may be. For Leo Pavia. For those great spirits – Montague, Monkhouse, Mair. For the loyalty and devotion of my friends everywhere. For the humble helpers who have made my work possible. For any talent I have possessed, and the gift of energy to prosecute it. For never having utterly lost the sense of the glory and the freshness of a dream. For never having for one instant believed that there hath passed away a glory from the earth."

Before coming to my life's end – perhaps at the close of a year, or on a birthday, or on a long, lone journey – it could be rewarding to make up such a list of one's own. It would, of course, be impossible to include all the good things up through the years, but there are many that should not be omitted. As one has said, at the end of pondering this matter, "*There are so many things that we have no right to forget!*" I think so, too. They are the stuff of which thanksgiving is made.

However commonplace, there is the air in one's lungs, the light in one's eyes, the perception of lasting values, the capacity to help one's fellows. And there are creative gifts, from God the Creator – though the result may be but a meat pie, succulent, with golden crust, set before a hungry family; a lawn beautifully mown, with tidy edges; an article for a favourite magazine, as honest and limpid as a mill stream; a book, a poem, a painting, a piece of graceful pottery.

I feel lastingly thankful that early on I was shown how to do many of these things with my hands; and, a little later, to serve across a country counter for six years, when people came from far and near in their traps, and everybody knew everybody. We worked long hours for little money; but Christmas Eves were like family festivals. We helped children and adults, one by one – concerned that they had so little to spend – sharing their secrets, so that we could waken on Christmas morning knowing what delights awaited stocking-openers across the friendly countryside. The anonymous modern checkout girl at the supermarket can't do that. And something real is lost. Nobody, when one goes for groceries, any longer enquires about "Mother's sciatica", or whether "young Tony was moved up to a new class after the exam"; or "whether Dad's early potatoes, that he spoke about, turned out as well as he had expected. People, in those days, were persons. Today there is not just a devaluation of money but a devaluation of personality. My work situation supplemented my constant solitary correspondence study by night. This led on, when my counter work ceased, after six years, to my acceptance for Deaconess training in a beautiful southern city which I grew to love.

This was followed by years of service in pioneer country parts; and later, by a grim social service experience in our largest city, during an economic crisis spread throughout the land. Many in our midst were without work – many even without the common decencies of life. Day after day, we had men and women forming queues for food.

And then I had to spend some years on my back, with an unusual heart condition resulting from a germ collected whilst handling old clothes in a Mission. That year, which spread into the next and the next, I owed my life to the skill and faithfulness of my doctor. And when at last I could walk with a stick, I went to his surgery to ask for a statement of my indebtedness – though I had not the least idea how I would meet it. (There was no Social Security in those days, and my cash was down to a couple of coins in a slim purse.)

My doctor, who had been to my bedside morning by morning for many months, looked at me for a moment in silence, then said, "*But there's no fee!* Between those of us involved in your case, there is not one but would say, 'By rights, you ought not to be here.'" After a further silence, he continued, "I'll tell you this as a medical man, *but for your Christian faith and spirit, you wouldn't be here.* And no doctor will take a fee for that." (I took my leave of him with tears brimming, that next moment must surely have fallen. A long time later, when I started doing light work for which I was paid, to express my thanks I selected for him a set of travel books that I knew he had mentioned with some eagerness.)

Still, I was far from working full days, and I wanted to use well the leisure that I still had to take. I wondered about a further correspondence course. But it was dear Rene's suggestion that most appealed – and at the same time brought me to my life's main ministry. *I began to write.* (Later, when I had settled down to tell briefly of that long, exacting time we had shared, I asked if I might submit my manuscript for the kindly doctor's scrutiny, lest I should have "improved upon the truth". He read it, thanking me, when he returned it, for what I had written, and actually questioned only one medical word there, for which together we found another.)

Life-long thanks were due to Rene in this connection, too, of course. I can't think that I ever *fully* expressed them – though we lived together, gardened together, read together, travelled together all fifty-two years, until her life ended. We built our home, "West Hills", together; and then it became essential to move to a level site, to our beloved flat by the sea, where I am still. We shared good world-friendships, some begun away back when we were first in London together; some later when we were in charge of an International Camp of young women from thirteen different countries. We had received my second book (the first published in London) during that visit, to be followed by very many others. Callers have since come from all over the world, and countless letters have crossed to and fro, enriching us both beyond all reckoning.

Though our first travel adventure was from one side of the world to the other, it was unbelievably inexpensive, compared with the cost of world travel today. For all that, our trip took a great deal of saving for – money was scarce in those days. I worked through my Summer holiday, running the first Auckland Methodist Health Camp for children – and I hoarded my modest pay like a squirrel. I sold some of the treasured books from my shelves; cut several friends' hair for sixpence a time, as they needed it done again and again; earmarked a small insurance due, which I had begun when a child from birds-nesting money earned from the Council responsible for protecting orchards; tram money saved by walking sections in the city; and a modest family gift that came enclosed in a letter from my father wishing me travelling mercies a day or two before we left.

Rene had already arranged happily for qualified friends to take over her music teaching till she returned. A quarter of the hard-earned sum we each needed went before we even started, in exchange charges. And that was painful – a hundred pounds took a lot of hard planning to gather! But reckoned against present travel rates, no one today will believe that in 1937 – which amongst extra unexpected delights, gave us the Coronation of George VI and his beloved Elizabeth, and many additional events all the rest of the year – we two travelled by sea, right round the world, for so very little.

Eagerly we joined the Youth Hostel Association, relatively new at that time, and, carrying our haversacks,

76

walked through the green loveliness of England's Spring
landscape, on into Summer, in such beautiful weather that
we never once put on our rain-capes. We slept every night
at a Youth Hostel for a shilling a night each. Imagine it –
twenty sleeps for a pound! This took us into castles, into
renovated cow barns, and into lovely historic weavers'
cottages, night after night. And many choice spirits whom
we met are close friends to this day – letters continually
crossing, tying our hearts together.

Much the same waited for us on walks through Scotland;
and later within Wales and Ireland. Each day's experience
seemed to have been possible just at the right time.

But changes were coming. We could not fail to wonder
what their nature would be. Hitler had not then laid his
stranglehold too firmly, though the first signs of soldiery in
the cities, forests and on the newly constructed auto-links
within various parts of Europe were painfully obvious. On
several occasions in Germany, the meal being served in an
eating-place was required to cease, and the company keep
silence when Hitler's voice came over the wireless. Several
times we saw him; several times heard him speak – or shall I
say "shriek"? One night in Munich we had to hand over our
passports at bedtime, but mercifully were able to collect them
in the morning. This was in 1938, the year when travellers
were bold enough to ask about the enormous chain of
factories beside the roads in the Ruhr, their tall chimney-
stacks pouring out a continuous volume of smoke. Someone
in our company one day at a meal table asked what they were
manufacturing – and was told *meccano sets for children*! My
friend and I might have been "green" but not that green! Next
year was 1939 – and happily, we were home!

*   *   *

Everywhere since, travellers have been at a loss to ignore hints
of war in their comings and goings, so easily can it spring up!

In one of my later books, I mentioned a morning arrival

in Lebanon – stopping off to see a friend, a vice-principal of a college, on our way to London. To our surprise, as dawn broke, a United Nations plane was on the tarmac. And as we made our way into the city, it was to find it held tight within the rules of Curfew. And at that early hour we were much aware of soldiers lying flat with their pointing tommyguns on the tops of main buildings we passed. And when the lifting of the Curfew later allowed our friend to come out to an agreed office to pick us up, it was to confess something she didn't like to tell us over the phone, that the College already had bomb-holes in the garden, and slates off its roof!

Next time I made my way to England and thought to stop off in Jerusalem – I'd never been there at that time, and felt I might never again be so near – it was to find Jordan and Israel, where I intended going to visit dear friends, separated by barbed-wire. I had need to show a second passport and set of documents which, from the Jordan side, their enemies had not handled or looked upon; and the same, in reverse, at the Israeli side! Do you wonder that on returning safely home, after these occasions, *I give true and lasting thanks* for safety in travel?

Many a time, over those same years, I had reason to join meaningfully with a congregation in the words of the General Thanksgiving: "Almighty God, Father of all mercies, we Thine unworthy servants *do give Thee most humble and hearty thanks* for all Thy goodness and loving-kindness. . . .

"We bless Thee for our creation, preservation, and all the blessings of this life" (all the blessings – that is more, much more, than the freshness of a pine forest that stirred Katherine Mansfield; the breath to breathe: cotton wool clouds sailing in the blue above: the bumbling velvet beauty of a bee: more even than the gifts and experiences we so often set our hearts on, and stand open-handed to receive. And much more than *things*), ". . . above all, for Thine

78

inestimable love in the redemption of the world by our Lord Jesus Christ; for the means of grace, and for the hope of glory.

"And, we beseech Thee, give us that due sense of all Thy mercies *that our hearts may be unfeignedly thankful*, and that we shew forth Thy praise, not only with our lips, but in our lives; by giving up ourselves to Thy service, and by walking before Thee in holiness and righteousness all our days; through Jesus Christ our Lord, to Whom with Thee and the Holy Ghost be all honour and glory, world without end. Amen!"

Apples – and Apples

My father taught me my alphabet in readiness for school. And it was only natural that he should begin with "A for Apples", for our Nelson district was fast becoming not only a cluster of orchards but the largest exporter of apples in the country. And it is blessed with many striking considerations: trees and gardens unmatched, no pollution, no traffic congestion, lovely lakes and rivers and sea shores, and an overall annual two thousand four hundred hours of bright sunshine!

Understandably, I've never lost my interest in apples. But I raised my eyebrows when lately the Rev. Jim Skett, from another sun-blessed, apple-producing part of the country, wrote to give me his permission to quote an arresting experience.

"One of the really great things about living in Napier," said he, "is the ready availability of fruit and vegetables. You can pick your own, buy from a stall, or fill a bag from a bin.

"A couple of weeks ago I went to get some apples from an orchard I hadn't been to before. The first thing that caught my eye, as I stopped the car, was a single tree growing alongside the driveway: it was an apple tree, but on it were over a hundred different kinds of apples. The orchardist had grafted on to that one tree different varieties from all over the world. A painted sign listed the varieties, and from the numbered tags on the tree one could identify them. There were one hundred and seventeen different varieties on that one tree! It quite fascinated me, and I've thought a lot about it since. (I didn't know there were so many kinds: I was familiar with the popular ones, but I couldn't have named a hundred and seventeen.)

"This particular tree is special enough – it ought to be mentioned in *The Guinness Book of Records*.

"I let my imagination play", said Jim Skett, "as I went on thinking about it. For instance, I wondered whether Paul the Apostle, if he'd seen it, might have added a further illustration to the pictures of the Church he gives at different points in his letters? He spoke about the Church as a family; sometimes, as a building; and sometimes, as a band of pilgrims. But his favourite picture of it was as a body, with its different parts all performing individual functions. '*Many members*,' he said, '*but one body*.' I wonder, would it have appealed to him to think of the Church as *one tree*, with many different varieties grafted into it?

"To become a member of the Church is rather like that. Jesus Himself talked of being the vine, and His disciples the branches. And each branch like that of the apple tree in Napier, drawing its life from the central source.

"Yet each branch of this tree", added Jim Skett, "*produces its own particular apple*. The life flow is expressed in slightly different ways in the fruit. And that, of course, is what happens in the Church: we're not all duplicates, and we misunderstand the Church completely if we try to make each other so. Living and serving together we provide a variation of our common life – *all Christians, but refreshingly different in our worship and life!*"

* * *

And that, I feel, is well said. From the start, surely, the God of infinite variety wouldn't have wanted it otherwise. I always find the New Testament Book of Acts exciting to read: "The disciples", it says, "were called Christians first in Antioch" (chapter 11:26). But they were very dissimilar.

"When the leaders of the church at Jerusalem", as Dr William Barclay reminded us, "got word of what was going

81

on at Antioch, they very naturally sent down to investigate the situation. And it was by the grace of God they sent the man they did send. They might have sent someone of a rigid and narrow mind who had made a god of the Law, and who was shackled by its rules and regulations. But they sent the man with the biggest heart in the church. They sent Barnabas. Barnabas had already stood by Paul, and sponsored him when all men suspected him (Acts 9:27).

"Barnabas had already given proof of his Christian love by his generosity to his needy brethren (Acts 4:36, 37). So when Barnabas came down to see what was happening, and when he saw *the Gentiles being swept into the fellowship of the church, he was glad*.

"Someone, he knew, had to be found to be put in charge of the work. That someone had to be a man who had a double tradition: he had to be a Jew, brought up in the Jewish tradition; but he needed to be a man who could meet the Gentiles on equal terms.

"For nine years or thereabouts we have no record of Paul. The last glimpse we have had of him, he was escaping by way of Caesarea to Tarsus (Acts 9:30). No doubt, for nine years he had been witnessing for Christ in his native town. He had been preparing himself, and now the task for which he had been destined was ready for him; and Barnabas . . . put him in charge of it." So the church was saved from stultifying dullness and sameness.

"The first thing Barnabas did when he got to Antioch," Professor G. H. C. Macgregor underlined for us, "was to remember Paul. He went to Tarsus and found Paul and brought him back to Antioch. And there they worked together . . . Within a year," he was happy to state, "they had the church established on firm ground, and by that time the people who belonged to the church were called for the first time 'Christians'. And there never has been a better name by which to describe the followers of Christ. We are not 'Catholic' or 'Protestant', 'Liberal' or 'Orthodox'. We are 'Christians', for all our dissimilarity, and in that descriptive name we find the common basis of our unity." (The name "Christian" itself was at first, of course, a half-jesting, contemptuous nickname, since the people of Antioch had a notable flair for that sort of thing. But soon the members of the Christian Church embraced their nickname, till in time all the world came to know it and hold it in honour. In much the same way, through the centuries following, other nicknames such as "Puritan" and "Methodist" and "Quaker" have won a place; but none matching that of "Christian".)

In my own Christian experience, again and again, I have marvelled to find myself, the world around, worshipping, serving and witnessing with others so diverse in their approach to Christ, and of so many nationalities and cultures. (I started to count and name them all, but gave it up.) God knows them – Roman Catholics, Anglicans, Methodists, Quakers, members of the Presbyterian Church, the Church of Scotland and the Dutch Reformed Church, and as many more. One of my experiences was to serve a year along with the Rev. Dr Raymond Dudley, born in Fiji, educated in Australia and New Zealand, and President of the Methodist Church of this country when I was elected. He was the *first* dark-skinned, handsome citizen elected to that high office of leadership. Nor must I forget a tall world editor friend of mine in the States, with deep devotional sensitivity; nor a principal of a well-known Christian college; nor yet another, a gentle, strong doctor of medicine. And my reverent, silent memory must fill in the others – many counting themselves of "lowly degree" – not forgetting a faithful pastor in Hong Kong; and a poor native leper woman with whom I worshipped miles out from Australia's northern city of Darwin. She lacked a hand to hold her half of the hymnbook we shared in a little hospital chapel. This, I tell myself with wonder, is the Christian Church in the world – *and I belong to it*! I do not love a part *against* the whole, for that is no occupation for a serious Christian; I love a part *within* the whole. A privilege indeed!

Recently I bought from my favourite bookshop a fat paperback by the late Rev. David Watson, who for sixteen youthful years served at St Michael-le-Belfry in York, where "the church has grown from a tiny handful, to a pioneering fellowship exploring new forms of worship". He titled this book *I Believe in the Church*, and began by saying on its first page: "This has been the most difficult book I have written! To begin with, where do you start or stop on a subject as vast as 'the Church'?"

On a later page, he underlined with wonder: "*The Christianity of today is far from dying or dead*. Approximately one thousand million, or one-third of the world's population, profess to follow Jesus Christ – more than double any other of the great religions. Some of the statistics, from the best-known available sources, would surprise many an unbeliever. In 1900, seven and a half per cent of the population of Africa were Christians; today the percentage is thirty-three per cent, expected to rise to fifty per cent by AD 2000. In Latin America the current growth of population is three per cent; yet amongst evangelical Christians alone the growth rate in recent years has been ten per cent. There are some seventy million Christians in Asia. In Indonesia, there have been over fifty thousand baptisms in five years.

"Far from Christianity being the last-ditch stand of middle-class culture in the West, in the last few years more than two hundred missionary societies have been founded in the Third World, with three thousand missionaries sent out."

At a certain season of the Christian year, I receive in this little country a pastoral letter from my minister, to keep my loyalty in focus. And I'm glad to have it. One began by reminding me of the *local* nature of my belonging, as well as the *worldwide* witness. The Rev. Leslie Clements spoke there of "the big church on the corner, with the tower, and the lovely organ, and the blue carpet and sanctuary drape. Yes, that's the local expression of the Church – the place we love, where we meet on Sundays. The place where our young people are lovingly launched into marriage; where their babies are brought for baptism, and from which with pride we carry our dead. It's also the place where regularly the Table is set with a 'fair cloth', and we celebrate the Holy Communion. Our church home, where the church family meets, and learns about Christian living, and where we say thanks to God for all His gifts to us.

"But," he had to add, and found pleasure in allowing me to quote here, "we belong to another Church, too. We can't visualize it so easily. We use grand words to describe it, like 'Holy Catholic (Universal) Church', 'the Body of Christ', 'the Bride of Christ'. We also use great words like 'the Church militant' and 'the Church triumphant'. We sing, 'And we on earth have union with God the Three in One, and mystic sweet communion with those whose rest is won.' (I often wonder what these words mean to a modern congregation – not given much to mysticism, or poetry for that matter – but without doubt those who coined these words were expressing a very deep experience and faith.)

"The local church is very necessary", he concluded. "Without it 'the Church Catholic' would not exist – and if you have no vision of that 'great Church', global in scope, spanning the centuries, reaching back to the beginning, and reaching forward into the future, then the local church loses its fascination. If you really believe that you belong to the glorious company of God's people everywhere, and in all times, you will be much less likely to give way to despair at the lack of progress. The church may at times look like a cosy meeting place, but it is much more than that, and I hope that all of us from time to time catch a glimpse of the true meaning of THE CHURCH."

This is the Christian Church in the world, in the present day! That is the great wonder – so diverse it is, so rich, so amazing – it sends my thoughts back to that apple tree in Napier.

So Catching

It is not always easy on a bus, a train, or a ship, to escape those earnest souls who want to tell you the story of their illnesses – without a single detail left out. (It has not, so far, happened to me on a plane: perhaps the faster form of trave accounts for that.)

I think I can claim that in the hazards of life, my heart is a sympathetic as any. But I must admit that ailments, past, present and prospective, are really not my favourite form o entertainment. On one occasion a friend did keep me glued in a cafeteria for a whole hour, while she told me of her influenza. Of course, influenza is interesting – but I have never found it that interesting!

I *was* fascinated when first I learned of its great age, and how it got its name. It seems it first appeared in Europe, during the Crusades, its nature credited with being an infliction of the stars and heavenly spaces. But more important, it was noticed how *the ailment spread from one sufferer to another, like an influence*. So it was named *influentia coeli*.

Who among us would want to relate to a stranger on a journey how we had suffered a miserable time in bed with "influence"? Its history in England is a little hazy, but it seems its agreed name goes back to Huxham, in 1767. The difficulty was eventually overcome by embracing the Italia name for influence, *influenza*. (That really sounded myster ous enough to boast about.)

By now, it seems, most of us have some painful knowledge of it – some of us several times over, though so far I can't think that I've ever boasted of it to a fellow traveller.

One mighty medical tome I consulted assured me that influenza had been responsible for twenty pandemics in the last two hundred and fifty years. (The most severe of which I have any living knowledge was just after the First World War. Many in our little country suffered its onslaught, and many died. I was not afflicted myself, but I still remember by name many neighbours and friends who were.)

Even in a light attack, there are few maladies so disagreeable as influenza, despite its interesting name and history.

* * *

No one of us, of course, lives to himself or herself: bad things, as well as good things, are passed on, though often unconsciously. These are actually St Paul's thoughts in one of his letters in our New Testament: "*None of us liveth to himself*" (Romans 14:7).

Looking back now over the path I have come, I am glad it is so, for great enrichment has come into my life this way. My late friend Dr William Barclay used to speak of "*the impossibility of isolation*" (he was commenting on those very words of St Paul's in Romans). "No man", he found himself translating, as thankfully as I do myself, "can disentangle himself either from his fellow men, or from God."

Then he added this in three tenses: "He cannot isolate himself from *the past*. No man is really a self-made man." "I am part", he quotes Ulysses as saying, "of all that I have met." "A man", my friend went on, "is a receiver of a tradition, of a heritage, of an heredity . . . True, he himself does something to that amalgam; but he does not start from nothing.

"And he cannot isolate himself from *the present*. We live in a civilization which is daily binding men more and

more closely together. There is nothing that a man can do
that can affect only himself . . ."

Nor is that all. My friend adds, "He cannot isolate
himself from *the future*. As a man receives life, so he hands
life on. He hands on to his children a heritage of physical
being, and of spiritual character. A man is not a self-
contained individual unit."

And that goes for each of us. We have to reckon with this
enduring thing I am calling "influenza", "influence"; for it
is far more telling in this realm than in what happens to the
body. In his review of H. E. Sheen's book, *Canon Peter
Green: A Biography of a Great Parish Priest*, Dr Barclay
was moved to write: "On any grounds, Peter Green was a
great man. At Cambridge he rowed for his college boat;
was President of the Union; and took a First in Moral
Theology. He was a King's Chaplain; he was offered the
bishoprics of New Guinea, of Lincoln, Birmingham and
Blackburn. He wrote almost forty books; and for forty
years and more contributed a column to the *Manchester
Guardian*. At his semi-jubilee in Salford the *Guardian* gave
him a leader, and the University a D.D.; later, Salford was
to make him a Freeman. When he had completed his
twenty-five years in St Philip's, Salford, the Dean of Manchester said of him: 'He is the greatest parish priest in
England. Yes, and more than that, he is the most human
parish priest in England.' . . .

"A boy at school, whose name we shall never know, was
a great influence upon him. This boy was brilliant neither at
studies nor at games, but he was known to be religious.
Young Green spoke to him about what religion meant to
him. At first the boy said the more or less conventional
things. Then quite suddenly he said: 'Do you really want to
know what religion is? Well, it's waking up in the middle of
the night and remembering that you belong to God, and
turning over and going to sleep happy because of it.'" But
it's much more than that!

Dr Elton Trueblood, a fine Christian leader of our day, questioned one by one a group of twenty-five laymen within the Church, about the major influence which had helped him into a satisfactory, committed faith. The striking thing was that every one of that company had to say that what had counted most was, not a book, nor a service, nor a lecture, nor a sermon – but *a person*!

I've often thought to try out that experiment myself. It would be a surprise if the issue came out differently. It is true, the gentle moulding of life is often unconscious. One of the best-remembered New Testament word pictures turns on the astonishment of two companies, at the end of life's day. "Lord," one group exclaimed, "when saw we thee an hungred, and fed thee? or thirsty, and gave thee drink? When saw we thee a stranger, and took thee in? or naked, and clothed thee?" And the King will say, in effect, *"All this was unconscious, as far as you knew; but to those of mine whom you served, it made all the difference"* (Matthew 25:37–40).

And "influence", or "influenza", if you can use the word in a spiritual sense, goes on. When Dr Donald Fraser came home from his missionary years in Central Africa, the native office bearers of the church sent him a word of thanks that surprised him greatly. It said that he had found them savage, and *had left them all greatly enriched*; he had introduced into their lives schools and churches, and coloured all their days with the beautiful fellowship of Christians. And they finished their communication tellingly: "We are now ashamed *where we have not caught the infection of a like heart*."

Influenza! This is part of the glory of the everlasting Kingdom. There may be some surprises for us, humble as we are, at the end of the day!

Inner Quiet

I couldn't help chuckling as I got out of my little car, basket in hand. "When you're out," my friend had said, "call at the poultry farm down the valley and get some eggs."

And right in front of my eyes now was a professionally painted notice: "*Quiet please. Hens at work!*"

I did not ask after the gentle humorist who put it there, but I wished I had the power to extend his concern to a score of places I know, where men and women work. *This is a noisy age*. Jets roar overhead; the grind of gears and thunder of wheeled traffic is with us most of our waking hours. Our sleep is all too often ruined by noisy adolescents on motorbikes climbing at speed. Road and street work in our city is accompanied by the stutter of pneumatic drills, and motor mowers at weekends ruin the quiet of our leafy suburbs.

Doctors and psychiatrists are continually telling us that noise is a contributing factor in the stress of our age. Neighbours' parties, radios and gramophones that waken us, produce extra toxins of fatigue which sleep is meant to neutralize. The medical journal, *The Lancet*, lately drew attention to this, and commented also on the risk many thoughtlessly run, in setting up homes near airports.

In great industrial cities, scientists have long been at work trying to discover *what sort of noise annoys most*. Rats exposed at close range to jet engines, they found, after sixty minutes died from a complication of internal injuries, including haemorrhages and atrophy of glands. And they reported this as a warning to us human beings. Duration is more damaging to some of us, it seems, than intensity; others are affected in exactly the opposite way. Some claim that they can raise their production output if they are allowed to work with a background of radio. I know an accountant who claims he can only add columns of figures if he has the radio going. One point on which he has not expressed an opinion, is *how long* he will be able to keep this up. I am not one who can work to background noises: I need quiet, even more urgently, I think, than any battery of hens!

"At twenty," says a royal physician, turning over this issue, "we scoff at quiet; at forty, we begin to think we need it; at sixty, we know we cannot do without it."

The quiet of the country into which many of us were born, was much more supportive than most of us realized at the time. It had a quality that did not call for absolute absence of sound. In the quietest of country places one was aware of the pleasant chirping of birds, the bursting of seedpods, the music of a stream over a pebbly bed – harmonious, natural, purposeful. The "rat-a-tat" of rain on a roof was another country sound we welcomed.

I was fortunate to grow up without knowing the word "decibel", that our city fathers today use so freely, and often with puckered brows. It wasn't in my *Concise Oxford Dictionary*, though it is in my more lately acquired *Britannica World Language Dictionary*. This defines it as "one tenth of a bel, the common unit of measure of loudness of sounds".

When I came to write a poem for publication in *The Listener*, I actually gave it the title, "Decibels". And there would be few, alas, if any, of the paper's modern readers who wouldn't know what it meant. I wrote:

Like Wind on the Grasses

Once, each day entered
    without knocking,
though childhood cherished
    its own sounds –
water running over
    grey gravel,
bird chatter in tall trees
    out-of-bounds.

When sun finished
    popping gorse pods,
and larks surrendered hold
    on the blue,
night summoned her cicada
    orchestra,
with sleep before the concert
    was through.

Now, day enters with
    grating gears,
while transistors bawl
    threatening ills;
jets rip the selvedge
    off the sky,
above a stutter of
    pneumatic drills.

R. F. S.

Quiet was everywhere at one time in this great northern city, on whose lovely rim I live. Now we have to seek out quiet. Fortunately we have countless beaches and parks, though even these at times are subject to the brashness of transistors.

I went, by invitation, a while ago, to lead a "Quiet Day" for the ladies of the Cathedral. Mid-morning we met in the tiny historic chapel of St Stephen. "It stands", to quote our modern *Mobil Guidebook*, "in an idyllic setting on a knoll overlooking Judges Bay and the trees of Parnell Park. It owes its existence to George Augustus Selwyn (1809–78), first Bishop of New Zealand. An earlier chapel than the lovely little one of today suffered collapse, because beach sand had been used in preparing its mortar. A storm proved too much for it. But its wooden successor has a special place in Anglican ecclesiastical history, as it was here in 1857 that the Constitution of the Church of the Province of New Zealand was signed on the table which now serves as the chapel's altar.

"Many of Auckland's pioneers and soldiers are buried in the churchyard, among them Bishop Cowie (first Bishop of Auckland) and the Rev. Rota Waitoa (the first Maori to be ordained)."

Today, the timbers of the little chapel are mellowed, its modest churchyard grassed over and lovingly tended. That morning, as we gathered, and then at midday took our lunch out of doors, the sweet smell of its newly cut grass rose to greet us.

Nobody but those of us involved in that "Quiet Day" came whilst we were there. Seldom have I donned my gown to lead worship, standing by such an historic altar, in a place so saturated with "holy quiet"! It was easy there to recall the words of the saintly Janet Stuart of long ago: "*Think glorious thoughts of God, and serve Him with a quiet mind.*"

Quietness is never just absence of sound, any more than stillness is absence of movement. The seasons in the country are always telling old tales, and making new promises; anyone observant knows this. Quietness and stillness are among God's great gifts, compounded and harmoniously purposeful. And so they are meant to be in human nature at its highest. To miss this secret is to run the risk of being nervously overwrought.

We can't all pack our bags and escape; though it is true that there come those times when the walls of office, shop and home seem to contract. We have to get away. Quiet of heart all the same depends on much more than just getting away. "Anonymous" showed himself a shallow fellow, without a divine secret, when he wrote:

> I would I were beneath a tree,
> A-sleeping in the shade,
> With all the bills I've got to pay
> Paid!

> I would I were beside the sea,
> Or sailing in a boat,
> With all the things I've got to write
> Wrote!

> I would I were on yonder hill,
> A-basking in the sun,
> With all the things I've got to do
> Done!

But a true holidaymaker *escapes to return refreshed*, – more than ever aware of life's true values. Holidays were once, in very truth, holy days; and they are still for many. The Psalmist led the way early, when he said, "I have calmed and quieted my soul" (Psalm 131:2; R.S.V.).

Florence Allshorn, possessed of many spiritual secrets, brought it into practice. Said she, in a letter to a friend fortunate enough to get away: "Do you know, I think one of the best things you can do on holiday is to ask nothing, want nothing, but just praise God for everything. Always be praising Him – for the little sticky leaves, the rich sombre greenness of the trees, all the kindness you get on a holiday. Just one long praise of little beautiful things, and forget that great big, blundering self of yours. *Then come back to us clean and fresh and courageous, and let us, too, get a sight of the glory of God!*"

A Voice in the Dark

I often wonder what effect constant radio news of war has on young children. My home was in the quiet countryside during the First World War. Each morning at school we saluted the flag, and felt very patriotic. We each did what was possible to help, knitting socks and balaclava caps for the men of the forces. I managed the caps – they were straightforward – but I must confess that it took me the *whole* war to get the two feet of my socks the same size. (But, of course, I wasn't very old.) My most constant job was to bowl my hoop two miles each tea time, and bring my parents the *Evening News*, tossed from the guard's van of the passing train. They wanted to learn how things were going at the front. (They told us children what little they thought we should try to understand; but it was very remote.)

The next war, in 1939, was different. I had just returned from twelve months overseas – part of that time spent in Germany and Italy, where it was all too easy to see and hear Hitler and Mussolini.

Soon, the importance of the newspaper gave way to *wireless news*, not once, but several times a day. And a number of our friends, just into their thirties, as well as neighbours and relations, were called into the forces.

"My father", said Father James Lyons of the Catholic Communications Centre, when those grim times were being recalled, "was a prisoner of war." Then in my hearing, he went on to speak of their joint troubles – his father, captured in North Africa and held in a prison camp in Bardia awaiting passage to Italy, and his family on the other side of the world, impatient for news.

It meant a very long time before it was all over and anxieties for dear ones could be dropped. Even then, "we never talked much about the experience," added Father Lyons, "but I remember him describing how frightening it was in the coldness and the blackness of the desert nights, knowing he wasn't free, and that the future was uncertain. The prisoners could call out each other's names during those pitch black times, and the sound of familiar voices was comforting. It seemed to 'soften' the night, make it more liveable.

Then Father Lyons went on to speak of John the Baptist, since it was the beginning of Advent. John was the "sent one" in the dark world before Christ came: he bore that name because he called people to repentance, and baptized them with water as a sign of their desire to live better lives. But John preferred a different title. When the people asked him, "Who are you? What have you to say for yourself?", he replied, "*I am a voice that cries in the wilderness*, 'Make a straight way for the Lord!'"

I knew what Father Lyons meant: it was "John the Voice" who broke into the frightening darkness of a world without an adequate experience of God, announcing an end to fear and the horror of feeling alone. He went on: "My father's experience in the prison camp has a new significance for me these days. The sound of human voices spoke to him of life, and of not being afraid, and of believing in the morrow. And it's not just prisoners of war or tenderfoot scouts who need those assurances. (Perhaps", he added, "you tremble at the thought of some darkened corridor in your own life. The voice of John is for you; Advent is for you, for each of us.) We constantly need the voice and presence of someone else – to share, and to dispel the fear."

I was grateful to Father Lyons for drawing my attention to this continuing reality, and for his readiness to allow me to quote him. Not many of us go through this life without finding ourselves at some time in "a dark place".

* * *

It was that way with Mary, carrying her spices, when Jesus died. "*When it was yet dark . . .*" we read of it, recorded in John's gospel (John 19:41–42; 20:1–16). It was not only that the morning had not yet come, following the shut-up time of grief and waiting for the Jewish sabbath to go by, as she prepared with loving care her part of the burial rites for the Beloved. Darkness lay over her heart and mind; a darkness many times more dreadful than that which lay over the land. Then, One at last confronted her – One Whom she took to be the gardener – there in that dark situation. And a voice spoke her name: "Mary!" "She turned herself, and saith unto him, 'Rabboni'; which is to say, 'Master'." And that made all the difference in the world! Life was not "dark" any longer for that loving, faithful woman.

Always, in dark places, ever since the Resurrection, men and women have shared with others news of the word and presence of Christ, risen and once more close, and so have witnessed to a like experience.

As the long years of the last European war dragged on, a minister in Surrey, Norman Cope, wrote a book which spoke to many beyond his own hard-pressed congregation. He called it *The Night is Ending*, and his editor kindly sent me a copy. When I had read it, I placed it on my shelf lest one day an experience of darkness should come to me. I marked lines in his Introduction which are still very relevant: "*The night is ending because the night does not belong to the eternal things; the day is dawning because light and love and purity are in the kingdom of the Father.*"

He did not, of course, make up this assurance. That

claim is but the *echo* of that chapter (20) of John's gospel – a glorious reality that any of us might lay hold of. And it seems today more than ever real as we face human darkness. It bears striking witness to the presence of Christ, the Son of God, in this world: "He was in the beginning with God; all things were made through Him, and without Him was not anything made that was made. In Him was life, and the life was the light of men. *The light shines in the darkness, and the darkness has not overcome it*" (John 1:2–5; R.S.V.).

This was He of Whom "John the Voice" told (verses 6–8 of this everlasting opening chapter of John's gospel): "There was a man sent from God, whose name was John. He came for testimony, to bear witness to the light, that all might believe through him. He was not the light, but came to bear witness to the light."

"But the climax", says the modern commentator in *The Interpreter's Bible*, "is not reached till verse 14, when the divine revelation is announced as the Incarnation of the Son of God." As plain as that, *for we need the delivering truth plainly stated when we find ourselves in a dark, frightening place. We must know, as plainly as Mary in the garden near the open tomb, Whose is the voice and presence!*

To make utterly certain that this need is met, Dr Goodspeed's rendering is, if anything, more straightforward: "The light is still shining in the darkness, for the darkness has never put it out." Men and women have borne witness to its reality in every generation. Bengt Sundkler records the certainty of an African soldier who, in the Second World War, found himself cruelly mocked by a British sergeant. Trapped together in a dark shell hole, the hard-bitten NCO turned to his mate with, "Let us see now what your God can do!" *And Christ, in His word of assurance, and His presence, did not fail him.*

Another, a German Christian, was imprisoned at the same time as Dietrich Bonhoeffer. One night, he was in despair. "Then," he was able to witness, "Christ Himself was in my cell, saying, 'Blessed are the poor in spirit; blessed are they that mourn; blessed are the meek . . .'" Asked later, "Is this true?", that needy Christian was able to say with great joy and peace, "*It is true!*"

And we ordinary folk, about our work, experiencing the pressures of ill health, family and community anxieties, or fears of world nuclear destruction, know we need this same help of a sustaining kind. The poet G. F. Bradby, in his little book *Through the Christian Year*, shares a prayer that I still find very meaningful:

> Teach me to know Thee, King of Kings,
>   All-loving, as all-wise,
> Not only in the lovely things,
> The trees, the flowers, the painted wings
>   Of birds and butterflies,
> In perfect sounds and perfect forms;
> *But in the darkness and the storms*
>   *That sweep through shattered skies;*
> *That in the thunder I may hear*
> *Thy glorious voice, O God, and feel no fear.*

Such Beauty!

Do you sometimes long to be a poet, a painter, a psalmist? I do. It is usually when some unexpected beauty is bursting from leaf, bud and blossom, and the day still young. Generally, I'm content to be a writer and speaker, and glad that my life is so rich. Awareness of beauty, and capacity to share it, I have come to realize, is not necessarily tied in with a vocation. It's much more a matter of spirit.

"Fiona Macleod" tells how unforgettably one morning Seumus, an old fisherman of the islands of the west, was standing still with his wide blue bonnet in his hand, the sun shining upon his mass of white hair, and his glad, still youthful eyes gazing lovingly upon the sea. "Morning after morning," the old man explained, "fair weather or foul, after I have risen from my prayers, and ere I have broken my fast, I come here . . . and bow my head with joy and thanksgiving before the beauty of the world."

I count him kin to the Psalmist, and wonder what time of day it was, or indeed what season of the year, when *he* cried from his heart, "*Let the beauty of the Lord our God be upon us*" (Psalm 90:17). He does not stop to tell us what his work was – only to relate the longing of his heart to the practical things of each day, unveiling his inmost heart to God: "Establish thou the work of our hands upon us; yea, the work of our hands establish thou it."

There are times, I find, as a lover of things beautiful, when God seems very close. *Beauty, then, isn't a pleasant extra, but a living essential.*

Beauty, of course, is one thing to one person, and something else quite different, if as meaningful, to another. God can minister to us, as to old Seumus, through the subtle moods of the sea; or He can speak through the beauty of grass and garden, or through some great mountain reaching upwards. Many forms of beauty, it pleases a practical person like myself to know, serve the ongoing pattern of life. The colour and fragrance of the commonest flowers attract bees, and so secure fertilization. But that ministry is not the sole purpose of their beauty. It doesn't completely cover the greening, undulating landscape; or the beauty of minute forms to be found in forest ways, still untrodden by the footsteps of man, and at the bottom of the deep sea pools the sun never reaches. Some of these are microscopically examined by experts, photographed, and reproduced in lovely volumes which find their way on to our public library shelves and on to our coffee tables, and we wonder at their amazing beauty.

Then there are everyday things we take for granted, like buttercups, with their beautiful, smiling, lacquered golden faces. Morning by morning, as I step through my open doorway to bring in the paper, I see a common daisy with a dewdrop in its eye. Some mornings there are sounds and shapes of life, matching the seasons, that I've known all my days. There are again and again tiny things of incredible beauty, that I can only examine by bending down. And there are great boughs, strong and bountiful against the blue of the sky. And there are beautiful silvery cloud patterns.

This Summer morning early, I find myself singing:

> O Lord, let me be aware –
>   quicken my heart to care
> for Your world; and each of us granted breath –
>   cast between birth and death –
> birds, at first light, greeting the day
>   *before small winds can say*
> *what can be said of life's wonder*
>   *here inexhaustible*!

R. F. S.

Why are so many things in God's world so beautiful? The complex propagation of life is not an answer great enough. The readiest answer has come to me, so far, from one of our modern scholars, Dr Herbert Farmer, and it is: "*Because God is a Lover!*" (As I listened to him delivering his lecture, other shafts of light enlarging this truth came to me, too.)

Many a time since, I've thought gratefully of Florence Allshorn, founder of "St Julian's" as a place of Christian refreshment of spirit. Someone wrote of her: "*She had a passion for beauty* . . . The world, for her, was charged with the grandeur of God." It was His creation, and she took endless delight in its manifold revelation . . . and in being a partner of God in the work of perfecting it. Both in the house and in the garden, she never tired of creating beauty. Her sensitive awareness could be seen in her choice of clothes, in her arrangement of a room, or of a tiny vase of flowers, in her love of pictures and books, of fine leather and hand-stamped papers, of fine embroidery, of a well-ironed traycloth, a clean scrubbed table, of a polished floor, of a carefully arranged dinner table, or a well-written letter, or of crisp overalls. "All of us", said one of her friends (and Dr J. H. Oldham gave it a deserved place in his biography of her), "saw how ceaseless her questing was, whether for that one perfect rose that transformed the flowers in the chapel, or for the placing of a picture to catch the light. She rejoiced in such signal triumphs over the ugly or the merely utilitarian." And another added, "She transformed what was commonplace to most of us, into a breathless adventure. It was exciting to arrange chairs in a sitting room with her, or saucepans in a kitchen, or to build a new rabbit hutch. Each detail held its significance because of its place in a larger vision – *to love into beauty* whatever she met, whether it was a soul or a material object."

Of course, we do not know the beauty of God here, till

we know that it is not alone in flowers on an otherwise bare embankment; in unguessed symmetry where no human eye sees; or even in the majesty of silver clouds piled high. *His greatest beauty awaits us in the mind and spirit of men and women*, because His greatest love is centred there!

I look to Jesus, walking this same earth, for an example of this beautiful mind and spirit. The New Testament furnishes me with countless examples – above all *the beauty of love, the beauty of obedience, and the beauty of caring*. These three were foremost in our Master's ministry.

I was reminded of this threefold essential in a quiet corner of Kent, as I walked alone one morning, complete with haversack. Spring had just reached little Elmsted, and beauty was throbbing at the heart of things. There, in the church, before the altar rails, I paused to examine a white memorial stone and read its inscription. It was simple enough, and rejoiced in the offering of Katherine Taylor's life: "*As grace*", it said, "*had filled her with inward beauty, so nature adorned her with outward comeliness.*"

The old saying that "beauty is skin deep" misses the mark. Katherine Taylor had a better sense of the meaning of the words Peter wrote to the Christian women of his day: "Your beauty should reside, not in outward adornment – the braiding of the hair, or jewellery, or dress – but in the inmost centre of your being, with its imperishable ornament, *a gentle quiet spirit*, which is of high value in the sight of God" (1 Peter 3:3–4; The New English Bible).

* * *

The first of the threefold expressions of beauty, seen so unforgettably in Jesus' life – *the beauty of love* – was nowhere, of course, better elaborated than in the gospels, and in Paul's immortal chapter (1 Corinthians 13:1–10; 14:1; Moffatt):

> I may speak with the tongues of men and of angels,
>   but if I have no love,
>   I am a noisy gong or a clanging cymbal;
> I may prophesy, fathom all mysteries
>   and secret lore,
> I may have such absolute faith that I can move
>   hills from their place,
>   but if I have no love,
>   I count for nothing;
> I may distribute all I possess in charity,
> I may give up my body to be burnt,
>   but if I have no love,
>   I make nothing of it.

"Love is very patient, very kind. Love knows no jealousy; love makes no parade, gives itself no airs, is never rude, never selfish, never irritated, never resentful; love is never glad when others go wrong; love is gladdened by goodness, always slow to expose, always eager to believe the best, always hopeful, always patient. Love never disappears.

"As for prophesying, it will be superseded; as for 'tongues', they will cease; as for knowledge, it will be superseded. For we only know bit by bit, and we only prophesy bit by bit; but when the perfect comes, the imperfect will be superseded . . . Make love your aim."

Scholars handling New Testament Greek help us to embrace for our everyday life what love really means – what beauty really means. They have a favourite word, *kalos*, which embraces both "good" and "beautiful". It is in this richest sense that I ponder the gospel record of our Lord, and rise in my pew from time to time to sing the opening verse of one of my favourite hymns:

Such Beauty!

Now let us see Thy beauty, Lord,
  As we have seen before;
And by Thy beauty quicken us
  To love Thee and adore.
    The Methodist Hymn Book

* * *

And there is *the beauty of caring*. I find more than one
author these days suggesting that we employ the word
"caring" in place of the better known word used by Paul in
1 Corinthians 13, translated "charity" or "love". It might
help us to grasp the word's reality, if we read "caring"
sometimes at that point in our private devotions. "Though
I speak with the tongues of men and of angels, *and do not
care*, I am become as sounding brass, or a tinkling
cymbal."

* * *

Said the famous Christian editor, Dr Robertson Nicoll,
speaking of our Lord and Master Jesus, "He did not
merely accept the will of God when it was brought to
Him . . . *He went out to meet that loving will, and fell on
its neck and kissed it.*"

We do not, any of us I fear, yet know the beauty of
obedience like that!

Happiness Can Be Had

It may surprise you, as it surprised me, to find that the lovely word "happiness" is not in our Authorized Version of the Bible. The word "blessedness" takes its place. One early character is translated as using both expressions in one sentence: Leah is caught up in a "spilling over of high spirits" at the prospect of a little new life being added to the family, and says, "*Happy* am I, for the daughters will call me *blessed*!" (Genesis 30:13).

A like "spilling over", for other reasons altogether, is known by most of us at some time or other. And we never forget it. A long-time poet friend of mine in Canada recently shared with me such a moment. Into my letter she slipped the following poem:

> See where the orchard trees link hands,
> link hands and, dancing, go nowhere
> beyond this bright exuberance
> of pleasure in the petalled air.
>
> I, too, have known *a happiness*
> sweep over me with so profound
> a music I was all a-dance,
> though rooted to the solid ground.
>
> R. H. Grenville

You know that feeling?

When our young Lord came, He was contrasted with the sterner John the Baptist. His bearing, and His words, were so different. "He began His ministry", as A. E. Whitham, one of His disciples of our day, liked to say, "*with a catalogue of happiness.*" (That is how he spoke of the Beatitudes; Matthew 5:3–11.)

In our Authorized Version, on which most of us were brought up, the word "blessed" appears right down the page, set out a little like a poem. But the word is not as close to our hearts today as the word "happy". In that respect the modern Good News Bible serves us better. It reads:

> Happy are those who know they are spiritually poor;
> the Kingdom of heaven belongs to them!
> Happy are those who mourn;
> God will comfort them!
> Happy are those who are humble;
> they will receive what God has promised!
> Happy are those whose greatest desire is to do
> what God requires;
> God will satisfy them fully!
> Happy are those who are merciful to others;
> God will be merciful to them!
> Happy are the pure in heart;
> they will see God!
> Happy are those who work for peace;
> God will call them his children!
> Happy are those who are persecuted because
> they do what God requires;
> the Kingdom of heaven belongs to them!

"Happy are you when people insult you and persecute you and tell all kinds of evil lies against you because you are my followers. Be happy and glad, for a great reward is kept for you in heaven. This is how the prophets who lived before you were persecuted."

Some time ago *Punch* offered a picture of a mother with her little brood at the beach. They were in a squabbling mood, and what was she saying? We were left in no doubt

– it was printed plainly at the bottom of the sketch: "I've brought you here to be *happy* – and *you've got to be happy!*" But that kind of interpretation of happiness isn't worth much. To start with, where children are concerned happiness is a state of going somewhere wholeheartedly. I've had a lot to do with taking other people's children to the beach, for a day's outing or as part of a summer camp. That is community service that I'm never likely to forget. My experience with other people's children, with mothers, and persons of all ages, persuades me that there is nowhere a slot machine where we can put in our small coins, and pull out a slab of happiness!

Many people nowadays, though blessed with brains, a pleasant personality, and good prospects for the future, seem unable to lay hold of happiness. This truth arrested me when I was last in London. One afternoon, after an hour with my editor, I walked on towards the eastern end of Fleet Street, that historic street of printing ink, to Ludgate Circus. And there, on the wall of a building, I came upon a memorial tablet set up in remembrance of Edgar Wallace, the widely read novelist. It seemed that, during his career, he had become a familiar figure thereabouts. Before he reached the end of his life, his biographer claimed, he had everything – money, fame, power. But there was one thing he did not achieve in those last years, and that was *personal happiness*. Somehow, that evaded him. And that late afternoon, I moved slowly from his memorial tablet, and went sadly on my way.

* * *

In a short time, however, my spirit had taken a steadier hold on things. "Happiness can be had", I wanted to tell the world, for I was myself a happy person. I've not till now set it down on paper, but while I'm doing so I want to say that happiness is not a superficial thing. It goes, if my experience through the years is anything to judge by, much deeper than another author's proffered "secret": Mark Twain claimed that "happiness is a knack like whistling through your fingers". But, as I have entered into it, with deep thanksgiving and wonder, to me it has seemed much more. Olive Schreiner's words, in her *Story of an African Farm*, speak more closely to me: "*Happiness is a great love, and much serving.*"

And this reality is confirmed in our day by many whom I have met or read about, who have become friends, or heroes and heroines. "*A happy life*", said my youthful hero, artist and doctor Edward Wilson, who died with Captain Scott in a small tent in the great white spaces, "*is not built up of tours abroad and pleasant holidays*"; though he embraced such experiences as gladly as any of us. He talked of wild flowers, in clumps beside the way, that "only those can see who have God's peace and love in their hearts . . . *So long*", he summed up, "*as I have stuck to nature, and the New Testament, I have only got happier and happier every day.*"

* * *

In a different Christian setting, I find another hero, Dr Wilfred Grenfell, writing to a young nursing sister from his place of "loving and serving" in Labrador: "Come and spend your vacation in our mission hospital. You won't get any pay, and you'll have to pay your own travelling expenses, *but I promise that you will be happier than you ever were in your life.*" And what came of it? That young nursing sister accepted; more than that – at the close of her vacation she wrote, "*You were right! Can I come back to stay?*"

* * *

This world of ours, God be thanked, is full of kindred souls who know this secret: "*Happiness is a great love, and much serving.*" Jan Struther was another. She gave us her little book *Mrs Miniver*, and helped some of us to stand an inch or two taller, in difficult times, in hard places; and with a great love and much serving. She wrote a striking poem, and at the end of her life it was read out, very thankfully and fittingly, at her funeral service:

> One day my life will end; and lest
> Some whim should prompt you to review it,
> Let her who knew the subject best
> Tell you the shortest way to do it.
> Then say, "*Here lies one doubly blest.*"
> Say, "*She was happy!*" Say, "*She knew it!*"

At the Heart of Things

I can hardly think of a family these days, where there is not a camera of some sort. All parents, it seems, want to keep a record of their young folk, from infancy up, and of their family holidays or more ambitious world travel. We have far out-distanced the modest "Brownie" that some of us once possessed, acquired after many birthdays and patient pleading. I can recall to this day how I studied its little booklet of instructions, never dreaming that, years on, a day would come when I would be able to circle the earth with a colour camera.

In many families nowadays, as Ruth Pidwell has had pleasure in assuring me out of her overseas experience, "there will be more than one camera". Then she felt she had to add, "Of course, the camera always lies! Think about the pretty girl on the cover of *Woman's Graphic*. She doesn't really have that much hair; there's a wind machine well out of sight of the camera, creating the illusion. (I myself never pose for a photograph without reaching for a comb, and a smile – not if I can help it! We all want only our best side put on record.)"

Then she went on: "Our family has been rather 'camera happy' in the past year. We've been living in Switzerland – surely the most photogenic country in the world. In fact, I think the camera lies least when it takes those chocolate-box pictures of the Alps, the lakes, the chalets with their geranium-filled window boxes, the incredibly manicured countryside, and the cowbells.

"One Sunday, our cameras were very busy as we took the train to the top of Mount Pilatus. This rack railway is,

111

I think, the steepest in the world, a one-in-two gradient. We rode up at that crazy angle, taking in distant snow-covered peaks, jutting above the prim and perfect countryside. We took picture after picture.

"At the top, we decided to take some shots of each other, to prove that we'd been there. 'A little to the left', came the instruction. 'No, wait, I'll go back. For goodness' sake, look this way!' (You know how it is, trying to get a family looking harmonious.) My husband placed our youngest daughter beside a fence at the edge of the summit, to get her silhouetted against the sky. Presently, 'Move from that old post,' we heard him say, 'we don't want that in the picture!'

"She moved to the left, and stood poised and perfect against the blue backdrop. The picture taken, we went down the slope a little way to the restaurant for coffee. And as we sat there, looking along the path we'd just taken, back to the summit, we all saw it at the same moment: standing there, metres high, just to the right of where Belinda had posed, *was a cross*!

"But not one of us, a minute or two before, had seen it for what it was. In the narrow viewfinder of the camera, seeking out a good picture, it was just an old post, irrelevant, ugly and intruding. We had tried to blot it out of our photograph.

"We often, it seems", Ruth Pidwell went on, "view life through the selective lens of a camera. We record pictures that are just not true. We don't like the world as it is – the wars, the suffering, the pain – so we focus our attention firmly on what is pleasant.

"Sometimes, for all that, we need to take an honest look, take in the whole scene before us; take a second, unbiased view which shows us that total reality includes more than mere beauty: *it includes pain with pleasure, darkness with light, death with life*. It has to, for life is like that. And so is God's love.

"These can only be fully understood when the cross is included in that picture!"

* * *

In this life, we cannot have Christianity without a cross – that's a certainty. "Our religion", as Chaplain J. Cyril Downes reminded us in *The Facts of the Faith*, written out of a grim prisoner of war background, "is an historical religion, based not on myth or poetry or speculation, but on fact. It would matter little to Buddhism or Confucianism if it could be proved conclusively that their founders had, in fact, never lived; there still remains the philosophy, the system of ethics, the rules of life for the modern disciple to learn and follow. But once the historicity of Jesus is questioned, then Christian faith must inevitably collapse. God's revelation is made known to His people in and through history; it is an incarnational religion from first to last."

And the cross is a vital part of that picture – it cannot be meaningful without it – although some amongst us might prefer to speak more of Jesus' attractiveness as a personality; His joy, as one Who found a great deal of it in His life on earth; His approachability; His compassion shown to the beggar by the wayside; His acceptance of hospitality in many a home; His teaching skills; His courage on the lake at night, when storms came up; His kindly notice of children; His healing gifts, extended freely and effectively again and again; and always, His steady eyes, with which He faced situations, dividing the false from the true! He was the good Friend; the strengthening Companion when grief descended, as to those on the way to Emmaus. From early boyhood He had learned the reality of grief, as well as life's delights, running on familiar hills with the wind in His hair. He had gained all too soon, from what He saw and from what He overheard

113

in anxious family talk, the painful meaning of a cross. One person thereabouts, known as "Judas of Galilee", sought desperately to overthrow the Romans; and in time, all along familiar winding hilly roadsides, crosses went up in full view of the lad of Nazareth. The outcome now of the raid upon the Roman arsenal at Sepphoris was no secret: on every hastily raised cross, grimly in view, a fellow countryman was hanged. (A cross was never, to Him, a jeweller's ornament in gold. Not at all! It represented the greatest, grimmest cost that loyal love could lay upon a man.)

As He grew, He found the deep consideration of it constantly with Him; even as He travelled with His disciples, camping with them out under the quiet stars, as they talked at bedtime around the dying embers of their fire. Within their hearing, on one occasion, He found courage to say, "If any man will come after me, let him deny himself, *and take up his cross*, and follow me. For whosoever will save his life shall lose it: and whosoever will lose his life for my sake shall find it" (Matthew 16:24–25).

The point came, of course, in Jesus' brief ministry, when He knew that He had but one choice – to be put to *silence* on the Good News of God, or to be put to *death*. Deep down, He knew what His choice must be; He had an everlasting Kingdom to serve! And not much time left in which to do all that was required of Him, in love, for the lasting redemption of man.

His own cross, as Dr George McLeod painfully reminded us, was in actuality more than a symbol nicely out of the way . . . much less, a sign on a cathedral altar between two candles. Rather was it raised between two thieves, and at a crossroad beyond a city wall, so cosmopolitan that the authorities had to write up His title in Hebrew, Latin and Greek – as if, today, one might choose German, English and Afrikaans. That cross tore

114

His young body, bowed His courageous head, and wrenched from Him a cry the world has never forgotten: "Father, into thy hands I commend my spirit" (Luke 23:46). For the God Whom He served was Father still, even there!

Nor has the world forgotten the sudden cry of the centurion whose business it was to see this dastardly deed done. He had seen many die, but this time it was different: "And he glorified God, saying, 'Certainly this was a righteous man.'"

And though nobody thought of it at first, soon a handful of those who loved Him best came to the tomb at dawn bringing burial spices – only to find themselves involved in the world's first glorious Easter, confirming His triumph! And that remains the way for us to look at the cross!

A Lively Attitude

To this hour, I owe much to a good man with music in his heart. In 1910, when he first copyrighted a tune of his making, I was but a child, my singing scarcely musical, my range limited to a handful of nursery rhymes. But a few years later I happened upon Sir Walford Davies' simple tune, and the words set to it from *The Sarum Primer*, dating away back to 1558. Though I didn't know that, of course, till later still, when I tramped to the site of Old Sarum, haversack on back. By then I had become familiar with all three – tune, words, and Amen – in my hymnbook at the church where I worshipped. Gladly and meaningfully I had learned to sing:

> God be in my head,
> And in my understanding;
> God be in mine eyes,
> And in my looking;
> God be in my mouth,
> And in my speaking;
> God be in my heart,
> And in my thinking;
> God be at mine end,
> And at my departing. Amen.

And ever since that tramping trip to Old Sarum, in the lovely country green of England, I have been grateful to that early anonymous Christian who fashioned it, and to Sir Walford Davies who later, inspired of God, sent his words soaring upwards in song.

Many of us now find it a well-established part of our devotional utterance, offered in wonder.

And that is not to forget the "Amen". I shall always remember the night I made my way to Gresham College in London, to hear Sir Walford, by then honoured Master of the King's Musick; organist of St George's, Windsor; Gresham Professor of Music in the City of London. (That was in 1937 – and he died four years later – so I count his talk one of life's timely privileges.) That night at Gresham College he taught us to sing its "Amen". "The 'Amen'", he said, "cannot be too good. It is an opportunity to embody the great Christian affirmations. In singing 'Amen' it is well to pretend you may never sing another, so *put everything into it!*"

I have never forgotten those words! How many of us, I wonder, sing "Amen" like that? In early times, the word carried a great deal of meaning. It was originally spoken or sung as an expression of solemn assent, chiefly in prayer, sometimes by an assembly, sometimes by an individual. And there were times when it was used, and repeated, as in Psalm 41:13 and Psalm 106:48, accompanied by a rubrical direction: "*Blessed be the Lord God of Israel from everlasting to everlasting: and let the people say, 'Amen!'*"

In time, "Amen" passed over from worship in the synagogue into the liturgical use of Christian congregations, and on through the centuries, down to us.

It is a full, rich word of splendid assent. It sums up exactly the phrase of deep meaning often on the lips of St Francis de Sales: "Yes, Father! Yes, and always Yes!" It is not a word ever to be lightly uttered, or absentmindedly; but one that springs from the heart, as Etienne Mattier showed, when from the darkness of a personal experience he cried: "No questions, Lord! No questions! *Only Amens!*"

To use this full, rich word properly, one's whole life needs to be behind it. That was why Charlotte Brontë was so pained to hear it upon the lips of her renegade brother,

Branwell. He was only thirty-one, but in their old rectory beside the church at Haworth (which I had the privilege of visiting, high up on the edge of the Yorkshire moors), he had been a cause of much family grief. He spent a great deal of time at the inn; the rest shared between dreams and drugs, and an incredible affection for a woman many years older. "He made the days heavy with anxiety," it was recorded of him, "and the nights hideous with revelry. He talked wildly when sober, and was not fit for anyone to live with, when drunk."

At last, a Sunday morning came when the family gathered round his bed. A crony with whom he had spent much time at the inn slipped away out of the room. The church bells, all knew, would soon be ringing for Morning Prayer. Branwell's father fell to his knees beside the bed; and as the old man prayed, to everyone's amazement, his rebellious son was heard to pray too.

Charlotte never forgot it. "I myself," said she, "with painful, mournful joy, heard him praying softly in his dying moment; and to the last prayer which my father offered at his bedside, he added, '*Amen*.' How unusual that word appeared on his lips, those who did not know him cannot conceive." She understood much of the rich content of "Amen": it was more, she knew, much more than merely a decent termination of prayer. It was a word of deep, glad assent. She was familiar with its widely interpreted meaning: "So be it!"; but on her brother's lips it was all wrong. Apart from having scoffed at religion, he had never given any part of his life over to the good, glad things of God.

* * *

St Paul uses the word "Amen" very strikingly. And thinking back to the ongoing ministry of Christ, especially reading our modern translations, our understanding of 2

118

Corinthians 1:20 (Revised Standard Version) is quite commanding: "For all the promises of God find their *Yes* in Him." And Phillips, in his version, renders those same words: "He is the divine *Yes*. Every promise of God finds its affirmation in Him, and through Him can be said the final *Amen*, to the glory of God."

John Stacey, in the preacher's handbook, *About Faith*, prepared for present-day use, leaves us in no doubt about its meaning. "The Cornish Methodists," he says, "who used to shout 'Amen, Amen!' in the middle of sermons, had got the sense of the word right. The rest of us who breathe it fervently at the *end* of prayers of intercession, have got it wrong. 'Amen' is a Hebrew word, and it means 'True! I confirm that; add my voice to what you are saying.' In other words, it is the liturgical version of the secular 'Hear, hear!'"

And that was what Sir Walford Davies had in mind when he spoke to us so eagerly that night at Gresham College: "In singing 'Amen' . . . *put everything into it!*"

Mend the Ten Commandments!

I have been glad to find, as I've gone through England, that many churches are blessed with the works of craftsmen. Some show a gentle sense of humour, and I'm glad about that too. I think God saw that we'd never get far without it. It is a mistake to think that because a thing is serious, we should be thinking about it seriously all the time. That is one way to lose a sense of proportion. God, I think, can teach us a good deal through fun. If that gift didn't come from Him, where indeed did it come from?

Miserere seats (misericords), quaintly carved, you must have noticed, are to be found in many ancient churches, hinting at understanding relaxations within strict monastic rule. During the day and night, set services were often long. So the presence of a small, but adequate, ledge under his choir seat, when tipped up, must have been welcome to many a weary man who still had to stand in worship, even when he was feeling exhausted.

Parish registers also yield treasure; and sometimes they, too, are unwittingly funny. I remember particularly two items in the churchwardens' books at Holy Trinity, Bungay. The first, bearing the date 1560, records "a book of ye commandments that was set up on ye wall, 1s.6d. By order of Queen Elizabeth". An interesting royal desire! A fair enough entry – and very cheap!

I can visualize it, because long, long after 1560 we had a painted replica on the wall of my first Sunday School. It had decorative capital letters at the beginning of each commandment. I couldn't then spell out all the words – some were long, and I was still young when I left that Anglican Sunday School for another much nearer home.

But I missed the golden edges of those two massive panels. After the first day at the little Wesleyan chapel, I returned home to report to my mother that "there was nothing to look at there, and nothing to learn by heart!"

I discovered, a year or so later, that the Ten Commandments could also be found "in my own black Bible" (Exodus 20).

* * *

The second entry in the churchwardens' book at Holy Trinity, Bungay, this one dated 1625, reads: "For mending ye X commandments, 18s.00"! It was not only amusing: it was disturbing!

There are, I know, lots of people among us today who would like to "*mend the Ten Commandments*". "*I am the Lord thy God . . . thou shalt have no other gods before me.*" "Rather out of date", I think I hear some retort. "We must have our new car; our telly; our Sunday visit to the seaside. Mend the Ten Commandments!"

"*Thou shalt not kill.*" "But what are we spending millions on nuclear weapons for? Mend the Ten Commandments!"

"*Thou shalt not commit adultery.*" "But that's old-fashioned, surely. Mend the Ten Commandments!"

Holy Trinity, Bungay, set up its commandments in the age of the *first* Queen Elizabeth. But in this bright reign of our beloved Elizabeth the *Second*, surely it is time for us to do some serious thinking about them? Yes, but not in the way these modern answers seem to suggest. The first thing that I do want to acknowledge, of course, is that the Ten Commandments, as we have them in Exodus (and in early church buildings, up on the wall), are all cast *in a negative mood*: "Thou shalt not!"

Jesus was brought up on the Old Testament – but when He came, things did not stay like that. He did not discard the old commandments; He cast His new commandments *in a positive mood*. Those on whom the ancient requirements had been laid were a bold lusty people, as cruelly selfish and muddled as many who get into our news today. They needed some guidelines. Referring to this, our Bible scholar Dr William Barclay commented: "When we look at the Ten Commandments, which are the essence and the foundation of all law, we can see that their whole meaning can be summed up in one word: *respect* – or, better still, reverence. Reverence for God, and for the name of God, reverence for God's day, respect for parents, respect for life, respect for property, respect for personality, respect for the truth, and for another person's good name, respect for oneself so that wrong desires may never master us – these are the fundamental principles of the Ten Commandments."

And he who forgets it will go on reading court reports of foolish and brutal behaviour, even if he doesn't get into disfavour himself. Jesus knew a great deal about life; and men and women who gathered to hear Him found Him saying, "Think not that I am come to destroy the law, or the prophets: *I am not come to destroy, but to fulfil.* For verily I say unto you, Till heaven and earth pass, one jot or one tittle shall in no wise pass from the law, till all be fulfilled. Whosoever therefore shall break one of these least commandments, and shall teach men so, he shall be called the least in the kingdom of heaven: but whosoever shall do and teach them, the same shall be called great in the kingdom of heaven" (Matthew 5:17–20). *He saw the law being fulfilled in a new spiritual quality; the negative becoming beautifully positive!*

Dr Arthur Cowan knew that he had to underline this to young men and women coming into the ministry of Christ and His Church. Their sermons on the Ten Commandments "had to point out their hitherto omissions – they had been concerned with *negative prohibitions*, not *posi-*

tive deeds. It was when the law was fulfilled in the Gospel, as Jesus said it was His purpose to make plain, that the most creative realities were to be seen. The Ten Commandments, as set down in Exodus 20, and in another version in Deuteronomy 5, held no mention of such qualities as love, forgiveness, self-sacrifice, and humility." These, of course, are the essence of the Gospel, as revealed by Christ – not of the law, given to men and women at the birthday of the world.

For years, in my earlier writing ministry, I contributed to a lively Canadian magazine. And there came a day when the editor felt that there was need to make these things, of which I am now writing, much clearer than he judged some of them to be. So he put forward the idea of having a competition among his readers. He headed it: "Are the Ten Commandments out of date?" A good many readers were young, newly involved with the hassles of the world, and they seized the opportunity and reached for their pens. And "senior citizens" leafed through back numbers of the magazine to see what was being said, as it was good they should; for the competition was centred round a subject that concerned all ages.

I liked best the contribution by one, till then unknown to me: the Rev. George G. Harris. "Psychologically, yes", he began, striding straight into the issue. "Negative prohibitions are known now to be less effective in directing human behaviour than positive suggestions." A good start! Then he went on to generalities: "Jesus did not hesitate to criticize the wording of the ancient commands. 'You have heard that it was said to the men of old time . . . but *I* say unto you . . .' In this He introduced a new era in religion. (Yet, the negativism of the Ten Commandments has clung to the garment of many a Christian, like old patches of cloth weakening the fabric of the new.)" Mr Harris went on to suggest that "a group of modern Christian scholars, *under the guidance of the Spirit*

123

of Christ, might agree on a decalogue for the young" –
and he composed there and then ten modern commandments himself. But you may feel that there is no need of
such things today, since we now have the loving commandment of Jesus, which He calls "the Great Commandment".

First, let me copy Mr Harris' modern commandments:

(1) You shall love the Lord your God with all your
    mind, heart, soul and strength, and your neighbour
    as yourself.
(2) You shall appreciate the wonder and beauty of all
    nature, the works of the Creator, and strive to
    picture them in forms of art, as they really are.
(3) You shall use the name of God in prayer, with
    reverence, truth, faith, hope and love.
(4) You shall set apart the day of our Lord's resurrection
    – the first day of the week – as individuals, families
    and communities, for rest, worship, healthful re-
    creation, charitable works, and friendly social con-
    tacts. And so far as possible, see that your fellow
    men enjoy the same opportunities for these blessings
    as yourself.
(5) Honour and love your parents, and your brothers and
    sisters, thus keeping family bonds strong and lasting.
(6) You shall always be faithful and affectionate to your
    wife or husband.
(7) You shall help your fellow men to live fuller and
    richer lives – to attain to what our Master called
    "abundance of life".
(8) You shall conduct your business or vocation in such a
    manner as to benefit not only yourself, but those you
    serve.
(9) You shall always speak the truth – whether in daily
    life, or on occasion in courts of law or on public
    platforms.

(10) You shall labour honestly and diligently . . . for yourself and your family, free of envy of the possessions of others, ever striving to do unto those others as you would have them do unto you.

What do you think of this modern elaboration? Is it too wordy? For Christianity, at heart, of course, is life – not an intellectual extra for those who like this kind of thing.

One, long ago, asked: "Master, which is *the greatest commandment* in the law?" Jesus said unto him, "*Thou shalt serve the Lord thy God with all thy heart, and with all thy soul, and with all thy mind. This is the first and great commandment. And the second is like unto it: Thou shalt love thy neighbour as thyself. On these two commandments hang all the law and the prophets*" (Matthew 22:36–40).

Do we need anything more? On another occasion, Jesus went briefly over the same ground: "*A new commandment I give unto you, That ye love one another; as I have loved you, that ye also love one another. By this shall all men know that ye are my disciples, if ye have love one to another*" (John 13:34–35).

This is both *positive* enough, surely, and *modern* enough!

Songs As We Go

I could hardly believe it. For some time, two friends stood with me on the roadside, at what we hoped was the right place. Presently, to our joy, a bus drew up. Grasping a handful of small coins, I mounted the steps and asked for "three return tickets to Bethlehem". Bethlehem! Imagine it!

As we journeyed on the five rising miles to the south, the little white houses of Bethlehem began to show up. Soon our bus stopped, and we stepped out, overlooking the very fields where, on a night the world has never forgotten, "shepherds watched their flocks". And every recollection of it has underlined the amazing fact that *when God's "Good News" came to the world, it was not in a sermon, but in a song!*

At first, these simple shepherds tending their sheep were afraid (Luke 2:9). But soon a heavenly host was singing a glorious and reassuring message, "praising God, and saying 'Glory to God in the highest, and on earth peace, good will toward men'" (vv. 13–14).

From that time till now, a song has held a central place in the proclamation of the Gospel, issuing in the Incarnation of the Christ Child. That, of course, is not only for those of us who follow Him, and with a handful of coins buy a "return ticket to Bethlehem". Percy Ainsworth, a well-known and sensitive young preacher among us, put it beautifully for all who could be reached by his words. He said, "When you watch religion at work, you see a morality; when you think deeply about it, you find a theology; but when you come to the very heart of it, you find *a song!*"

Later than the events associated with Bethlehem, when Jesus had shared his last meal and intimate talk with His disciples in the Upper Room, the gospel record says: "And when they had sung an hymn, they went out into the mount of Olives" (Matthew 26:30).

Christian song continued to sound a triumphant note, when the dark days of the mock trial and crucifixion were over, and Christ had gloriously risen from the dead.

The most remarkable thing about "this new sect", Pliny reported to the emperor during that first Christian century, was that "they kept singing in their little meeting places – kept singing hymns to Christ as God".

Clement of Alexandria, in the second century, had the same resounding story to tell, not only of their gathering together in worship, but of their singing in the homes and fields as well. "Holding festival, then," he said, "in our whole life, we cultivate our fields, praising; we sail the sea, hymning." And later, Jerome similarly said, "The plowman at his plow, sings his joyful hallelujahs!" "All come together with us to sing," adds Chrysostom, "and in it they unitedly join, the young and the old, the rich and the poor; women and men, slaves and free, all send forth one melody!"

How surprising must have been *this growing crescendo of song through the centuries*! Many others, besides these great ones, must have taken note of this witness of the Christians, often against an extremely difficult background.

Nearer our own time, Coventry Patmore set down what he judged to be the heart of it, and his words still ring out: "All realities sing – and nothing else will!"

It began, of course, as I have said, with the Incarnation, the coming into this world of the Christ Child. Nothing like it had been possible in Old Testament times – for all that the faithful raised their voices to God's glory. The period of the Psalms covered many centuries, and many experiences; so, like all songs, they showed change as they matched human need, and were shared. That is a reality we must hold in mind, as we rejoice in ongoing song-making by believers today.

Richard Crashaw's words, in his day, thrilled many a one. As Christmas drew near, they sang:

> Welcome! all Wonders in one sight!
> Eternity shut in a span,
> Summer in Winter, day in night,
> Heaven in earth, and God in man.
> Great little One! Whose all-embracing birth
> Lifts earth to heaven, stoops heav'n to earth!

Those words to this day rally many a songster. And what could better express the joy and wonder of newly acquired faith!

Charles Wesley, brother of John, scholar-evangelist, turned the hearts of many to his Lord and Master through his songs. John preached more sermons, indoors and out, than any other man using the English tongue, history tells us, and rode more miles on horseback to do so. But all the time, praises poured from his brother, making him the most prolific hymnwriter ever. In all, he wrote thousands of hymns. Not all have survived to this day, but a great many have. Glorifying God, along with those great Christians in other branches of the Church, the Wesleyans (later known to us as the Methodist Church) came into being – "born in song"! To match the need of the times, John Wesley added a Preface to the hymnbook he published. Various small collections had been turned into circulation by one and another, but nothing anywhere so embracing before. He was obliged to add, by way of explanation, "The greater part of the people, being poor, are not able to purchase so many books; and those that have purchased them are, as it were, bewildered in the immense variety."

And today, fresh compilations still come, though the Gospel of the Living Christ remains unchanged, since He is "the same yesterday, today, and for ever". But the social situation in which we find ourselves, and the living language in which we most naturally express ourselves, must find new wording to be effective.

Hymns have a wonderful way of binding together, not only the men and women of ongoing centuries, but of different denominations and nationalities. In the book which I use Sunday by Sunday (bearing a copy of that historic Preface from John Wesley) we have not only a rich number of Wesley hymns, but some classics of a much earlier time, and many that have been added since. Among them is one of my favourites, written by Saint Francis of Assisi all that long time ago: "All creatures of our God and King, Lift up your voice and with us sing, 'Alleluia, Alleluia!'"

It would be a thousand pities to lose such treasures, with our mania for modernity. Another of those we value, coming from many denominations and nationalities, is that great hymn from Martin Luther, a German who lived from 1483 to 1546: "A safe stronghold our God is still." There have been occasions in our lifetime when, personally and nationally, we have desperately needed that assurance.

Across another span of time, and from France, has come to us Theodore Monod's hymn with a sob in it: "Oh the bitter shame and sorrow, That a time could ever be, When I let the Saviour's pity Plead in vain, and proudly answered, 'All of self, and one of Thee'" (1836–1921).

In turn, from England, Henry Francis Lyte has given us one we could not be without: "Abide with me; fast falls the eventide; The darkness deepens; Lord, with me abide" (1793–1847).

Closely following it in time is one from across the Atlantic, from the pen and heart of Washington Gladden:

"O Master, let me walk with Thee, In lowly paths of service free" (1836–1918).

Nor must I bypass one of my favourites which I can never sing too often, given to our collection by Narayan Vaman Tilak, from India: "One who is all unfit to count as scholar in Thy school, Thou of Thy love hast named a friend – O kindness wonderful!" (1862–1919).

* * *

One of the most widely and deeply loved is, of course, Charles Wesley's "Jesu, Lover of my soul" – written as from an Anglican (1707–1788).

And one of my teenage treasures must be mentioned: "Dear Lord and Father of mankind, Forgive our foolish ways" – from John Greenleaf Whittier, a faithful Quaker (1807–1892).

I want to give thanks, too, for a much loved hymn from a Catholic heart, "Lead, kindly Light" by Cardinal Newman (1801–1890).

Another that we Christians in all denominations sing, is a gift from the Congregational Church: Thomas Binney's "Eternal Light! Eternal Light!" (1798–1874).

And we must not overlook the offering of Gerhard Tersteegen, from the Old Lutheran Church: "Lo, God is here! Let us adore" (1697–1769).

A hymn dear to many of us is "Blest be the tie that binds Our hearts in Christian love" which comes to us from a Baptist minister, Dr John Fawcett (1740–1817).

I could go on, but finally I must take space to include one of the first I learned to love, Cecil Frances Alexander's "There is a green hill far away, Without a city wall, Where the dear Lord was crucified, Who died to save us all." The author, who was from the Episcopal Church, lived from 1823 to 1895. Three years after our world received this universally loved hymn, she married, and her husband became Primate of All Ireland.

* * *

New hymns, of course, are still being written, coming to us in many forms, and of varied worth. One who enriched my anthology, *Delight Upon Delight*, is the Rev. Frederick Pratt Green, a gifted modern hymnwriter. In a letter, he shared with me the creator's joy at being asked to take a girls' choir to sing a selection of his hymns in Westminster Abbey. "Though it was a weekday service," he wrote, "the nave was filled, with people standing. It was a marvellous experience, the singing of the Farrington's School Choir. Magnificent!"

Does this mean that new hymns will be written, and sung, for ever? I think so, don't you?

* * *

Archbishop Anthony Bloom – to whom I acknowledge the keynote of this book on the title page, about the wind blowing, and being refreshed – has shared our present world long enough to know that it's a world of ups and downs. But he says: "Even people who believe half-heartedly can turn to thank God when something nice comes their way; there are *moments of elation when everyone can sing to God!*"

Seeking a Safe Place

It couldn't always have been easy, in early times, owning treasure – far from it. Only a few pieces could go into a locked chest, bound in hammered patterns of iron (and that was a great advance on still earlier days). Those families who had a trustworthy steward to look after such things were fortunate, though many an anxious brow, and many a strained back, resulted. But what could an owner of treasure do? Sometimes, a hole in the ground served, dug hastily while nobody was looking. It was resourcefulness of this kind, probably, that allowed the astonished peasant in Jesus' story to stumble on treasure (Matthew 13:44).

A crisis of a communal kind, like the surprise invasion of enemy forces, could "blow up" more than once in a lifetime, and call for quick action. If, as did happen, the master of the house or his steward were taken prisoner, or killed, treasure which had been buried could be lost for centuries, or for ever. Something of this kind could have happened at Mildenhall!

One afternoon, I was fortunate enough to be free in London, and I treated myself to a view of what had been found in quiet Suffolk. The very possibility of it fascinated me. By that time, the recovered treasure – thirty-four pieces of ancient silver – had been carefully cleaned, and mounted against a velvety piece of museum wall. A glorious sight!

A few days later, driving my little car, I headed for Suffolk, where I'd never been before. The afternoon was fine, and my heart was joyful in anticipation. Green countryside spun by. Seventy-six miles from London, my map said, and I thought, "I must be nearly there!"

132

Suddenly, I came upon a hedger-and-ditcher, an old man slashing into roadside nettles. Of course, I pulled up. "Nice afternoon!" I greeted him. "Can you tell me the way to Mildenhall?"

He pushed back his cloth cap, and purposefully said: "Go on another two miles. You can't miss it. You'll come to a field of barley. It's at a corner. I know the man who made the 'find' – went to school with him!"

"Really?" I responded.

But two miles on, I could see no barley – only a field of sugarbeet. And in it was a workman with his dog. I made my way across on foot, keeping a wary eye on the dog. "He won't hurt you", his master reassured me; but I felt happier when he was called to heel.

"I'm looking for the field hereabouts", I said, "where they found the Mildenhall treasure. Can you help me?"

"Ma'am," came his astonishing reply, "you're standin' right in it!"

"Are you the owner?" was my natural question.

"Well, I am now," came his answer, "but my old dad was then."

And he went on to tell me how, together, they had ploughed that field for years, until they had decided to engage Mr Ford's ploughman to do it, and go a little deeper. Then the "find" was made. That little extra had made all the difference!

The astonished ploughman immediately covered up his "find", as well he might, hardly knowing what to do. Then, after dark, his master and men came out with lanterns and sacks, and took it in.

"It sounds like the old Bible story", I suggested. "You know – 'treasure hidden in a field'. And to think", I added, "that it was so little damaged, after sixteen centuries!" I went on to tell him of my pleasure in seeing it as it now was, in the museum: the dish with the beaded edge measuring twenty-three and three-quarters of an inch across and weighing eighteen and a quarter pounds; all beautiful silver, with heads of dolphins protruding from King Neptune's hair; with patterns of gods and satyrs riding on the backs of sea monsters. And the platters, and the large Nielo dish, and the deep bowl with its cover, and the lesser bowls, and the little ladles, and the slender spoons. Thirty-four pieces! "You'll have to forgive me my enthusiasm", I said. "Here I am telling you. You've seen them, of course."

But no, he hadn't. At first, the "finders" had kept it quiet, not rightly knowing what to do. Then, when the police came, saying that it was to be reckoned "treasure trove", it was taken away into safe keeping.

Many of us today can take full advantage of banks and safe deposits – although, of course, there are certain types of treasures that we do not wish to put there, and some that we cannot.

If you are ever able to visit New York Avenue Presbyterian Church in Washington, D.C., you will be interested to pause in the vestibule to examine one of the church's treasures. You will be told that it is beyond price. It could be kept in a bank, or safe deposit, but they prefer to keep it where people can share it, and that is good. It is a letter written by Abraham Lincoln, and it is kept there in a special glass case which, I am told, cost two thousand dollars and is dust-proof, rust-proof, moth-proof, damp-proof, fire-proof, and burglar-proof! (You'll forgive me for mentioning this, but it's not the church's greatest treasure. *That* is the age-old Christian Gospel. And no glass case is adequate for that: *indeed, our only way of keeping it, is in giving it away!*)

Both Paul and Timothy understood all that is involved in this. The senior, more experienced missionary wrote to his young friend as he was setting out on his life's work: "*Keep the securities of the faith intact*"; and again, as being above all things important: "*Keep the great securities of your faith intact*" (1 Timothy 6:20 and 2 Timothy 1:14; Moffatt).

Timothy was left in no doubt about how this could be done: Paul's own example was ever before him. And now it is before *us*, all these centuries later, as we read what is recorded in such a thrilling way, for our inspiration, in the Book of Acts. My late friend, Dr William Barclay, began his little paperback study from the Saint Andrew Press, Edinburgh, with the words: "In one sense it is true to say that the Book of Acts is the most important book in the New Testament. It is the simple truth that if we did not possess the Book of Acts we would have, apart from what we could glean or deduce from the letters of Paul, no information whatever about the early Church. There are two ways of writing history. There is the way of the annalist, in which an attempt is made to trace the course of events from week to week and from day to day; and there is the way in which a writer, as it were, opens a series of windows and gives us vivid glimpses of the great moments and personalities of any period. The second way is the way of the Book of Acts."

But in his book *The Parables of the Gospels and Their Meaning for Today*, Dr Hugh Martin is fascinated by the treasures hid in the field. "Of what does this Christian treasure consist?" he asks, concerning the treasure held in the world today by the Church, and by you and me as Christians. And he answers confidently: "Peace with God; forgiveness; a sense of purpose and meaning in a life that before was futile; good will toward men – in a word, the knowledge of God. That, says Jesus, is the greatest of all treasures."

Some of us try to give it away in teaching, some in preaching, some in authorship, but there are scores of other ways besides. One of the most original, and effective, was that chosen by Kathleen Scotter, Superintendent of the Burwood Girls' Centre, a home for delinquent girls in our country. "Here," said my minister friend, Ashleigh Petch, in telling me of it, "Christian love, which is at the heart of sharing, came alive for many a one. When a girl had been especially recalcitrant, Miss Scotter would place a stretcher bed outside the room she occupied, and sleep there – always on call if the girl was fearful or tearful, until it got through to her that she was loved. And for millions of our fellow human beings," Ashleigh added, "all of them loved by God, people for whom Christ died and rose, there can be no awareness that they belong in any meaningful way, until they too experience love in action."

Our world waits here and now for men and women like us to grasp this glorious truth. *One by one, we each need to find his own way, her own way, to deal with our greatest treasure.*

To find how to give it away!

This Round World

I'm glad the world is round. I know, each time I set off from home, that some day, just as eagerly, I'll be back. And when that happens, like every other traveller, I'll be saying, "*Look what I found!*" I am not a great collector of souvenirs; rather a collector of experiences!

In this, I like to think I have a distant kinship with St Paul, that indefatigable traveller. I can't imagine him stuffing his bag of tent-making tools with "bits and pieces". But I know he greatly rejoiced in "finds" of which he could tell. When I was in Athens, I turned up my New Testament Book of Acts, to read again of his visit there; and what I read interested me so much (Acts 17:22 ff). "Then Paul stood in the midst of Mars' hill [just where I was standing at that very moment, a modern traveller, and where Paul's words are set up today in beautiful Greek], and said: 'Ye men of Athens, I perceive that in all things ye are too superstitious. For as I passed by, and beheld your devotions, *I found* [there is that traveller's word] an altar with this inscription, TO THE UNKNOWN GOD. Whom therefore ye ignorantly worship, him declare I unto you.

"'God that made the world and all things therein, seeing that he is Lord of heaven and earth, dwelleth not in temples made with hands; neither is worshipped with men's hands, as though he needed any thing, seeing he giveth to all life, and breath, and all things; and hath made of one blood all nations of men for to dwell on all the face of the earth, and hath determined the times before appointed, and the bounds of their habitation . . . for in him we live, and move, and have our being; as certain also of your own poets have said, For we are also his offspring.'"

I cannot speak for their poets, but I know, through my reading of the Old Testament, that many of His early prophets knew little of God. Amos, the prophet, could only speak of Him as the God of *justice*. That was away back in the middle of the eighth century before Christ. And it was a needed revelation.

Then, with the passing of time, came Hosea, speaking of the God of Whom many knew almost nothing. His broadening message was that, added to His *justice*, was His *mercy*. But still that was not a full delineation. That, in its fulness, needed time.

Presently came the voice of Isaiah, whose call to God's service was one of the most beautiful: "In the year that King Uzziah died I saw also the Lord sitting upon a throne, high and lifted up, and his train filled the temple. Above it stood the seraphims: each one had six wings; with twain he covered his face, and with twain he covered his feet, and with twain he did fly. And one cried unto another, and said, 'Holy, holy, holy, is the Lord of hosts: the whole earth is full of his glory.' And the posts of the door moved at the voice of him that cried, and the house was filled with smoke. Then said I, 'Woe is me! for I am undone; because I am a man of unclean lips, and I dwell in the midst of a people of unclean lips: for mine eyes have seen the King, the Lord of hosts.' Then flew one of the seraphims unto me, having a live coal in his hand, which he had taken with the tongs from off the altar: and he laid it upon my mouth, and said, 'Lo, this hath touched thy lips; and thine iniquity is taken away, and thy sin purged.' Also I heard the voice of the Lord, saying, 'Whom shall I send, and who will go for us?' Then said I, 'Here am I; send me'" (Isaiah 6:1–9).

But the vision of God revealed in this remarkable engagement seems, to me, very remote – as He must have

138

seemed, at the time, to lots of people. Seraphim, with wings that covered what was not to be seen! Well, no! Speaking for myself, I've never had any dealings with seraphim. Nor can I visualize God on a throne, high and lifted up, and His train filling the whole place. He seems so far outside our human lives; so majestic; so absolute; so spiritual! Despite what the earlier prophets had said of Him – of His *justice* and His *mercy*. Isaiah's main message was of His *holiness*. But how were ordinary people to grasp that?

And so the problem of the unknown God remained, high and lifted up.

* * *

Then came the Incarnation. God Who had been distant, and difficult to know, was no longer that way. Something had happened! "*When the fulness of the time was come*," to use the much simpler statement preserved for us in the New Testament letter to the Galatians (4:4), "*God sent forth his Son, made of woman . . . to redeem.*" There were no seraphim; it was all much more down to earth. Unbelievably, it happened, in the words of a modern poet:

> In a crowded public house, in occupied territory,
> where there was no room for anybody extra
> and rations were scanty . . .

A workman by the name of Joseph, and his young wife, were the chief actors, and a handful of nameless shepherds, working late at their job. Certainly, in time, other men, honoured as "wise men", appeared on the scene, bearing gifts of gold, frankincense and myrrh (and we find a place for three of them, suitably garbed, in our colourful Christmas pageants).

Like Wind on the Grasses

As a traveller to London, I went a while ago to a service at the Chapel Royal. I had had to get permission to go to that very small chapel, and for this had sought the offices of the Lord Chamberlain. To the service was brought from the town's oldest pharmacy, in St James's Street, *a small package of frankincense* and *two ounces of myrrh*. To these were added *twenty-five golden sovereigns* – the whole *representing the Queen's gift*. She was not there in person; only the one who bore it as her deputy. At five minutes before eleven I took my seat; and soon the chapel, lacking in itself stained glass and colour, quickened to glorious life with the arrival of the Yeomen of the Guard, clad in Tudor scarlet and gold, with the Queen's Chaplain, also in scarlet. Hymns, prayers, and scripture reading recalled the original gifts of the Wise Men. I'll never forget it!

This, of course, represented only part of that greatest happening of all time which we call "the Incarnation". It was more fully represented in what I later *found* (there's that lovely traveller's word again) in Tewkesbury Abbey that Spring. The charming old town, I knew, owed its name to Theoc or Theuk, a hermit. By the year 1102, an abbot and fifty monks were at work and worship on this piece of holy ground.

Everything, as I entered, proclaimed the abbey's age: its glorious tower, its massive pillars, fan vaulting, and sense of unity. Three women were at that moment setting armfuls of blossoming branches in bowls beside the pillars.

But until recently the thing that prompted my thanksgiving for the Incarnation did not exist. For centuries, the beautiful carvings in the high roof had been uncomfortable to look at, and were therefore generally unseen. But now, beside where the women worked with the flowering branches, set in the floor was a great mirror. Instead of craning my neck to see what was too high for human eyes,

I looked down and saw clearly what I sought. "Look what I've found", I said to Rene. "Has it ever been done before?"

The answer was "Of course!" It was what God chose to do at Bethlehem, so that there and then, for all time, the distant became near, and the indistinct known. So we gave thanks for "His dear Son . . . the image of the invisible God" (Colossians 1:13, 15).

"Philip saith unto him [what many men and women down through the centuries have repeated, expressing their deepest longing], 'Lord, shew us the Father, and it sufficeth us.' Jesus saith unto him, 'Have I been so long time with you, and yet hast thou not known me, Philip? *He that hath seen me hath seen the Father* . . . Believest thou not that I am in the Father, and the Father in me? The words that I speak unto you I speak not of myself: but the Father that dwelleth in me, he doeth the works. Believe me that I am in the Father, and the Father in me: or else believe me for the very works' sake'" (John 14:8–11).

The word "Incarnation" that we use, is a religious word meaning "an embodiment in human flesh". In the telling comment of the late Dr William Temple, the beloved and youthful archbishop of our lifetime, we hear it spun out when he says: "*The central fundamental affirmation of the Christian religion is that Jesus is the unique, final manifestation of God.*"

And the very humblest "traveller" amongst us, in this round world, who makes that "find", is rich indeed!

Needful Refreshment

When I hear men and women boast of wealth and popularity, I straightway boast of my love of fresh water – wells, streams, rivers!

It began for me, in early school holiday time, when my old bewhiskered grandfather took me by the hand and led me down beyond his little picket gate, into a grassy orchard. A well was there, the first I ever saw, surrounded by tufts of grass, golden buttercups, and mint. It was a sweet place! In season, we went with a basket to collect apples from the mossy trees; but daily, we went to the well. I never once went alone: the latch had always to be kept on the little gate.

I did not then know that a well is one of the most ancient things in this world. But later I read of Jacob's well, and of the hot midday when Jesus came to it. And years later I went to it myself.

It was already ancient when Jesus came there. In the East, cities rise and fall, roads and footpaths get covered over and lost under windblown sands; but wells remain, served by underground springs, though many names change through the centuries. The well of Sychar, dug by Jacob and his servants, is now approached by the modern Askar, a village in the valley about half a mile between two mountains and about a mile north of the well.

Though dug with simple tools, it goes down to an exceptional depth, as the woman with whom Jesus talked that day beside the well hinted: "The well is deep, and you have nothing to draw with" (John 4:11; R.S.V.). An old priest, in a shabby black robe and cylindrical headpiece, bade me let down his vessel at the end of a rope and see

142

how deep it was. Certainly it seemed a long time before there came the sensation of it touching the water, and there was a knack in tipping it, so that it might fill. Then, together, we hauled it up.

I recalled how Jesus had revealed His humanity there. He was thirsty. Travelling with His men, He had been hours on the dusty road; now hungry, they had gone into the nearby village to seek food. So He fully expected to be a little while alone, and perhaps welcomed that. But it was not to be. A woman was there: she had come at that odd hour to draw water when she had reason to believe the other women wouldn't be there. They didn't speak to her – only spoke about her! She had a reputation.

But Jesus treated her as a person, for all that she was a Samaritan, one of a despised people. And a woman! She was surprised to see Him there, for as a traveller He could have taken another way, the whole country was so narrow and so small. Galilee lay to the north; in the extreme south lay Judaea; with Samaria in between. There was no forgetting the centuries-old feud between the Jews and the Samaritans. Most did all they could to avoid meeting; but Jesus had His reasons for taking the way He chose through Samaria. (And our Christian world has rejoiced ever since that He did, for our gospels would have been altogether poorer without that meeting at Sychar's well.)

Although the encounter *started with a human request from a thirsty man, it went on to an unexpected life-refreshing talk of worship and "the living water".* Humanity's need, it was plain, was for more than water from a deep well: it was for spiritual refreshment that would never leave one wanting again. So it need not surprise us, in that story of Sychar's well, to find the Master moving from a request for a drink to talk of worship. For both ministered refreshment!

* * *

Since we men and women are made as we are, it is foolish to spend more of our time on the one than on the other. Of course,

> Water is a lovely thing,
> Dark and ripply in a spring,
> In a well, a simple gift,
> But, for all this, not enough!
>
> Anon

Most of us these days draw water so easily, and spend little time thinking about it. A tap is at arm's length, in the kitchen, the bathroom, the garden. It is rare in well-watered England, least of all in the Cotswolds, to come upon a housewife with cares about water. But I did one morning. She was carrying two empty pails, which she set down near a spring for a moment while we talked. She dreamed, she said, of some day moving to a city, or to some good handy town, where there was "water laid on". Where she lived most people still depended on a spring, pump or well. I could not forget her as I went on my way, along the banks of the little river, lipping gently. I fell in love with the Windrush, especially where its beautiful waters touched splendid barns and stone houses, on its way through quiet fields, untroubled by any event save the immemorial toil of the seasons, claiming man and beast. (Or so it seemed to me.)

I came to village after village, to Ford, and Temple Guiting, to Kineton, and Guiting Power, reaching Naunton – many a place blessed with trees, the scene showing itself in such gentle guise that I was afraid to look away for a moment, lest it should dissolve itself like a dream into a pleasant nothingness. Nowhere is it more beautiful to one who loves such things than where it divides the two Barringtons; and at Burford, the old, substantially bridged town where I have often stayed.

But the Windrush has many moods, flowing placidly through the meads, beyond which the graceful houses of a village rise, often with a church and gabled manor house; as when I turned towards Minster Lovel. For a moment my ear was reached by the rushing sound of hurrying water, though only for a moment: despite its name, the Windrush is a singularly placid stream. Here its waters are dammed to make a mill stream that, along with the old mill house, enhances the beauty of the village. With thatched roofs above handsome stone, it is a scene unforgettably beautiful. And there are great trees with waters lapping green banks, laughing under bridges, trying the patience of old fishermen, and teasing small boys with things to float. Such a river, apart from supplying water to drink, assumes the personality of a friend.

And it is refreshing, as are so many of God's gifts to us. Plainly, He does not want us to grow weary, dispirited, without hope. *His world has much to refresh us*: water, the beauties of nature, friendship, good books, music, art, meals – so many gifts for which we can be everlastingly thankful!

* * *

Amongst the saddest sights that I've come upon in my world travels, are the all too common crowded, parched, dust-blown areas without water. I've seen them in ancient parts of the world where there are shabby, hot, dusty refugee camps. And one of the private privileges of my life, when I came back from one of those journeys, was, along with Rene, to be allowed to pay for the sinking of a well in one such miserable centre of crowded life.

An experienced servant of Christian Aid, John McLeod, had spoken of the provision of water as a miracle that God had meant us all to enjoy. In his work, a modern deep-drilling rig could leave in a needy place a necklace of wells, spelling *refreshment*: "We drive up to a dry field," he said, "where the dust is blowing all about. In ten minutes we are ready to bore.

"First of all, the rock chippings and clouds of white rock dust are blasted away. After two hours we have got down to about forty feet. Then the dust stops, and water comes out instead. We have to keep on drilling to about a hundred feet, to get a sure supply of water; but even in solid rock, that takes only about a day. It really is nothing short of a miracle; and I believe in miracles, especially of this kind.

"For drinking water, we put a pump in the bore and seal the top of the hole. The people then have a supply of germfree water, something that has not happened in these villages for the last four thousand years."

Imagine it!

* * *

In one of St Paul's letters, he says a lovely thing about some friends, and gives us their names: Stephanas, Fortunatus, Achaicus (1 Corinthians 16:17), but he doesn't tell us exactly what they did for him. We can only guess: that they offered him hospitality; gave him a cool drink of water in a thirsty moment; lent him a treasured book to read; told him a story of courage? We don't know; but he said of them a glorious thing that any of us, in our giving, might covet. He said, "*They refreshed my spirit!*"

The Many-splendoured Thing

It's a long time now since I experienced such a wild, stormy night. I don't know how long I had been asleep when suddenly I wakened. I switched on the light above my bed, and as quickly as I could, closed the windows. A sleepy glance at my watch told me it was twenty past two. The wind and the rain were competing with a dark, desperate energy.

I read for an hour or two; then, when the storm seemed to be easing, I put out the light once more, offering a brief prayer for those at sea, in the air, and journeying on the roads.

* * *

And now, hours on, here I am awake a second time. The world, it seems, is in a completely different mood – my room flooded in sunshine. I reach for my wrap lying over the back of a chair, and with some eagerness rise and hasten to the kitchen to make a cup of tea. It is Wednesday, and my first thoughts are of the date, and what I planned to do today.

How often life is like this! God believes in "the second chance": He has done so from the beginning. And that of course is the glory of young Jacob's discovery, after rushing off following on a quarrel at home. That night, worn and troubled, he slept fitfully, his head upon a stone. A vast loneliness surrounded him in that solitary place, and he dreamed. It seemed that a ladder reached up between earth and heaven (suggested, some have felt, by the piles of stones about him in that place as fearfully he fell asleep). God, he had been brought up to believe, was away back with his people, in his ancestral home, and he felt terribly distant from Him. But he was wrong: that ladder, linking earth with heaven, meant something. "And Jacob awaked out of his sleep," the old Genesis record runs, "and he said, 'Surely the Lord is in this place; and I knew it not'" (Genesis 28:16). But he knew it now: it was a new beginning. (And many of us, outside the holy pages of scripture, have come to know what that means.)

We can't do without it; it is something that we rejoice in, as we do in sunshine after a frightening night. And as we do when we waken to a new day, and find we can go on in a way that we'd never guessed.

The Old Testament pages are full of experiences like that; and what discoveries can match them? Francis Thompson, one of our poets, after pondering over young Jacob's experience, and matching it with his own as one of London's ne'er-do-wells till his new day dawned, wrote of it in these unforgettable words:

> The angels keep their ancient places –
> Turn but a stone and start a wing!
> 'Tis ye, 'tis your estrangèd faces,
> That miss the many-splendoured thing.
>
> But (when so sad thou canst not sadder)
> Cry; and upon thy so sore loss
> Shall shine the traffic of Jacob's ladder,
> Pitched betwixt heaven and Charing Cross.

I have passed many times through Charing Cross – not only a well-known London area but in one's world of the spirit the symbol of a second chance. Wherever we stay, we can have a sense of the ever-present, forgiving God. So, being human, we rejoice in what we can learn of Him, just where we are. The "many-splendoured thing" comes to us because God takes the initiative. It is from His side, not ours, that comes the experience of forgiveness, issuing in the New Day! All our efforts to effect this by our own merits fail. "Even penitence," writes Dr J. S. Stewart, "without which pardoning love cannot become operative, is God-created . . . It is God's goodness and love, especially as these are manifested in Jesus, which evoke the penitence."

Many of us speak all too lightly of forgiveness – between God and ourselves, and between ourselves and our fellows. It seems to us a good idea, until there is something to forgive! Then, it is seen to be something more than an easy indifference, a flabby forgetting of what lies between two parties. For forgiveness is, at heart, a deep matter of relationship: costly to the Father, through Jesus Christ, and costly to the offender. And, as Jesus made plain in His story of the prodigal, there is in this new relationship that which brings in "the brother" also (Luke 15:11).

Our Lord taught His disciples to pray, recognizing this: "If ye forgive men their trespasses, your heavenly Father will also forgive you: but if ye forgive not men their trespasses, neither will your Father forgive your trespasses" (Matthew 6:14–15). With this comment, He made the family obligation unmistakable. *God's heavenly forgiveness and our earthly forgiveness are now for ever joined, and no man can put them asunder.*

Of course, our readiness to forgive is not *the cause* of our Father's forgiveness, but it is *the mood in which it becomes effective.* Hearts that harbour fault-finding, indifference, and hate, are in no fit state to receive the forgiveness of the Father. So we must learn to pray, "Forgive us . . . as we forgive." This is the only key that fits the "family life" which we share as people on this earth. It is not easy, but we cannot manage without it. Following the cry for bread, that our Lord taught His followers to pray, is this cry for forgiveness. And how right it is! For what is life for the body, if the spirit is estranged?

Forgiveness springs out of love, the "many-splendoured thing". "*Once there is love*," Dr William Temple was wont to say, "*forgiveness does not mean remission of penalty, but restoration to intimacy.*" This is the reality that those of us who read our New Testament give thanks for. There, in his letter to the Ephesians (chapter 4:32), we have Paul's splendid Christian summing up: "Be ye kind one to another, tenderhearted, *forgiving one another, even as God for Christ's sake hath forgiven you.*"

Promises Are a Problem

If you've ever been out in a little tippy boat when the sun has gone and the winds have risen, you'll know what Peter and Andrew and Jesus' other fishermen friends felt like. The Sea of Galilee, as I discovered when I crossed it in a small boat, is six hundred feet below sea level, and storms get up there very quickly. One minute, sea and sky can be friendly and calm; the next, they show a very different mood, striking fear into the hearts of even experienced fishermen. When Mark in his gospel relates the happening on the lake (Mark 4:36–41), he is describing a very dramatic occurrence. That particular boat and its crew had very often been out overnight: they were not amateurs. They knew all too well that the numerous ravines to the northeast and east could "debouch upon the upper part of the little lake", to quote one of our present-day writers. There were dangerous defiles in which the winds from the heights of Hauran, the plateaux of Trachonitis, and the summit of Hermon, could be caught and compressed in such a way that, rushing with tremendous force through a narrow space and then released, they could suddenly strike the lake.

But Galilee is not the only stretch of water where sturdy fishermen get frightened. In the Adriatic Sea, where two long rivers empty themselves, there is a part sometimes as smooth as Galilee, and sometimes as rough, and here little boats get whipped mercilessly and bashed about.

A story they tell there is about a fisherman whose home was at Perast, on the shore of a nice bay. Perast was bigger then than it is now, when only about a hundred people remain and some of its buildings are in ruins. But it is interesting still. On one of two tiny islands in the bay you can see a church with a spire; the other island has a church too, but it's the one with the spire that is particularly interesting. The fisherman in my story put out one day in his little boat and, like those friends of Jesus, found himself cut off when a terrible storm blew up. He had been in storms again and again through the years, but this time he was at a loss to know what to do. The winds howling down from the mountains continued stronger and wilder. More and more waves splashed into his small boat and, though he baled as hard as he could, it appeared that at any moment he might be swamped.

And what did he do? What many another in a fix has done: *he prayed. He promised God that if He would bring him safely back to land, he would build a little church on the rock to which he clung at that moment, when his boat foundered.* It wasn't actually big enough for a church, though big enough, as he found to his relief, for a half-drowned man to cling to.

God heard his prayer and answered. When morning broke, calm came after the storm and he was still alive. His fishermen friends rowed out and found him, and brought him safely in.

It is common for people who make promises to God when they're in trouble to forget them completely when things are right once more; but our fisherman wasn't like that. When his friends came out to get him, the first thing he did was to tell them of his promise. And they said, "We'll help you keep it!" In what time they could spare from their work, they filled their boats with stone and ferried it out to the rock. It wasn't easy. The first load they discharged sank clean out of sight, but they kept going, as they had promised. And in time, together they carried out enough to transform the rock into a little island, big enough for the building of a small church with a spire!

If you should ever go to Perast, the people there will tell you this story.

In the early part of the Bible we find these words: *"You*

must be careful to perform any promise you have made with your lips, anything you have freely and openly vowed to the Eternal your God" (Deuteronomy 23:23; Moffatt). So honest is the Bible in handling truth that it is plain that over a long stretch of time promises have been a problem. "Let me get over this accident," one will say, "and I'll never again be missing from my pew on Sunday." Another fashions her own promise: "Save the marriage of my daughter, and keep them close together, O God, and I'll never forget a decent contribution to missions." And a teenager, applying for a first job, prays as earnestly, "God, let me get this – You easily can – and I'll make it up to You! I promise!"

This matter of promises is so natural that the Church, in many of its most sacred services, makes provision for them – promises that, if kept, will enrich life ever after.

It all started, of course, with God Himself. In the very first book of the Bible, Jacob raised his voice concerning a crisis, *that* early in human history: "God of my father Abraham," he prayed, "God of my father Isaac, O Eternal who didst say to me, 'Return to your country and your kindred, and I will do you good' . . ." (What a promise!) (Genesis 32:9; Moffatt).

And out of plain honesty, Jacob had to go on: "I do not deserve all the kindness and loyalty with which thou hast treated thy servant; stick in hand I crossed the Jordan here, and now I am two companies!"

Other moments of crisis would come, *but there would always be his God, the God of his ancestors, Who kept His promises*. Before long, Jacob is fashioning another crisis prayer: "O save me from the power of my brother, from Esau! I am afraid of him attacking me and overpowering me, slaying our women and children. *Thou didst promise*, 'I will indeed do you good, and make your descendants like the sand of the sea, past counting for number.'" And that, for Jacob, as for many another of us, journeying through this life, was a wonderful reality. Any promise of God would be unquestionably honoured!

Nearer our own time we have Peter who, knowing God's Son, Jesus Christ, was able to write confidently to his fellow believers: "Peter, a servant and apostle of Jesus Christ, to those who have been allotted a faith of equal privilege with ours, by the equity of our God and saviour Jesus Christ; grace and peace be multiplied to you by the knowledge of our Lord. Inasmuch as His power divine has bestowed upon us every requisite for life and godliness by the knowledge of Him who called us to His own glory and excellence – bestowing on us thereby *promises precious and supreme* . . ." (2 Peter 1:1–4; Moffatt).

As the faithful fisherman of Perast discovered, there are always two participants in this essential undertaking. It is good that each one of us can sing:

> O Jesus, I have promised
>   To serve Thee to the end;
> Be Thou for ever with me,
>   My Master and my Friend:
> I shall not fear the battle
>   If Thou art by my side,
> Nor wander from the pathway
>   If Thou wilt be my Guide
>   *Methodist Hymn Book*

Twin Secrets

Monday, once again, is almost at a close. I have just 'phoned my friend and minister – which I don't do very often, of set purpose. I hoped he wouldn't think I'd over-looked his right to some leisure on a Monday; even less, that I'd learned of some tragedy in the parish. It was in fact neither. My question centred on his "recreational love"; I wanted to ask whether he had been away to golf that morning. "No," he had to reply, "as it happened, I was called to Jury service at the Court." (He is a hard-working man, and I think he needs to have his Mondays free. Finding the opportunity for his favourite sport is never easy – it requires him to rise early and join his fellow golfer, a retired college principal.)

A question had been raised during our earlier talk together; now I had another, springing out of a brief holiday he had shared with his wife in Britain. I asked, "Did you manage to get up to St Andrews?" His answer this time was enthusiastic: "Yes, we did!" Momentarily forgetting that I'm not a golfer myself, he went on to talk about the eighteenth hole.

St Andrews, with its historic buildings and monastic ruins, I knew, of course, to have much more than "the eighteenth hole". Undergraduates, in their splendid scarlet gowns, are a feature of its life. And shop windows have lovely woollen goods to offer. Others have travel books. And a few doors down, others offer brogues, others golf clubs and bags.

Golf in St Andrews assumes for many almost "a religious significance", and the "Royal and Ancient" has an atmosphere all its own. "Foremost among the treasures of

St Andrews", wrote one of my favourite travel writers, H. V. Morton, before I'd made my first journey "in search of Scotland", "is the silver cup given in 1754 by 'certain noblemen and gentlemen being admirers of the ancient and beautiful exercise of the golf', who each contributed five shillings to the first St Andrews' trophy. Then comes the gold medal given in 1837 by William IV, who endowed the club with the title of 'Royal and Ancient'. Golf, oddly, was spelt on this medal 'golph' – the error presumably of some uncivilized London goldsmith!"

When next I am sharing some leisure talk with my minister, I must show him what I have written about our 'phone call, because I want to quote him, and for the sake of author's good manners, must have his permission.

And I want to share, when he's got a few minutes, my favourite golfing story of St Andrews, which I treasure. It centres on the widely known and respected golfer, Bobby Jones. Twenty-odd years ago now, St Andrews conferred on him the Freedom of the City. Unhappily, this honour was left over long, so that by the time the ceremony could be performed, Bobby Jones was an old man in a wheelchair, deformed by some miserable pain.

But for many it was a memorable afternoon, and for one little eight-year-old girl especially. Pushing in through the crowd, she shyly presented herself and her programme to the honoured guest, and along with it a pencil, making the desire of her heart clear. And the great man was not slow to grasp it. Taking her programme in one hand, and her pencil in the other, despite twisted fingers he wrote gladly, "For Linda, in friendship: R. T. Jones."

Then – and this is the "twin secret of greatness", for *he was not only a giver, but a receiver* – he dug into his pocket and brought out for the little girl his own pen and programme, and said as he handed them over, "Now you do one for me!" And she did.

Can you imagine what that meant to both; and to those

who, like myself, got to hear about it? For it is in giving *and* receiving, I think, that we see greatness. It is not alone in one or the other.

Through the years I have read many times, from end to end, the New Testament Book of Acts – to me, one of the most exciting books of action in the world. But I must confess that there is one statement there with which I've never been at ease (chapter 20:35): "Remember the words of the Lord Jesus, how He said, 'It is more blessed to give than to receive.'" (Did He really say that? I've often wondered.)

It's a curious thing, if those *were* His words, passed on by some hearer to Dr Luke, writer of the Book of Acts, and felt by him to be worthy of preservation, that they nowhere appear in the gospels. There Jesus is seen purposefully passing on His life-giving truths; but we don't find these words which in the Book of Acts are attributed to Him. I have never before spoken or written of this perplexity of mine; but I've come upon a comment in *The Interpreter's Bible*, saying very much the same thing. It seems to me, looking at the New Testament that I've loved and trusted through the years, that a more credible portrait of Jesus comes alive, not by *separating* giving and receiving, but by *putting them together*, as He so gloriously did in His life and ministry.

I find it a very thrilling adventure to go through the pages of the gospels finding instances of those two life-enriching actions. In the life and ministry of Jesus, they stand out: *receiving and giving* were paramount from beginning to end. There is no forgetting the New Testament record of that wedding in Cana: His being there made all the difference to the young village couple and their parents and friends. From the start, He was a good receiver, and a good giver.

When He came back to Nazareth, where He grew up and people knew Him, we find Him on the Sabbath setting off to worship in the synagogue, "as His custom was". He was no longer a young local carpenter; it was still the same small village, and there must have been some things about that local worship that He might have criticized, even laughed at, as eager young men are inclined to do. But He was ready to accept whatever inspiration and challenge could come to Him there.

Out with His men, still early in their training, He found Himself very thirsty one midday, as they cut across Samaria and came to Sychar. The others went off to buy food and He, left alone, approached the woman by the well-side, of whom we have already spoken, and asked her for a drink. She was amazed that He would accept it, since she was a Samaritan – and a woman at that!

You will find it rewarding to seek out for yourself, in the gospels, such typical instances of His gracious spirit. Be sure not to miss that day during a crowded preaching period, with the people pressing about Him, when He was prepared to accept a singularly humble pulpit: Peter's fishing boat, pushed out a bit from the land. (Did it still smell of fish I wonder. I can think of one or two young preachers who might have thought it beneath their dignity – but He did not!)

And, of course, there was that robe He wore, that "seamless robe", a beautiful thing, as it is recorded. Somebody made it. Was it Mary, His mother? If so, she would have seen the soldiers, as a reward for their duty at the cross, toss for its possession. It was too good to cut, and go shares. Or was it made, with careful stitchery, by one of the other women? We don't know. But of one thing we can be certain: whoever made it, He *accepted* it!

And even after death, He had not changed. At the end of the day, after companying with a couple of troubled men part of the way out to Emmaus, He accepted their bread, and brake it, sharing a simple meal together with them.

* * *

But I will leave you to complete the adventure, to leaf through your gospels and ponder again instances of His *giving*. For they belong with those few of His *receiving* that I have cited, and the many more you will find when you set out on this adventure.

There are no stories of His giving money or possessions, which *we* usually think of when we are challenged to give. He had neither. His giving was physical and mental wholeness, and above all spiritual wholeness following forgiveness. Lepers, cut off from community, church and family life, were made new; blind beggars given the rich possession of sight; cripples enabled to fling aside their crutches – all of them, and more, singing praises to God!

And this amazing generosity of the Master goes on. He gives us, by His Spirit, here and now, for the enrichment of our lives as we follow, the "twin secrets" He cherished, that led Him into full life, great and good!

We are not puppets moved by a conjurer's finger.
We are greater than all the stars and all the suns
and all the greatness we have fashioned for
   ourselves.
For we are His sons and daughters and dear to His
   heart.
Wasn't that why He sent us His Christ?
Isn't that why He's always sharing His Spirit with us?
                              The Quiet Heart
                              Alistair MacLean

p 9 Holy Spirit

p 39 Poem

p 50, 52, 55

p54 Trinity ?

57 assisi

p64 recognition

p75 RS illness & recovery

p78 prayer p99

'Only at chess,' Noel put in.

'Dennis getting done,' repeated Norrie.' J. Espie in the sandhills with L. Wallace and me with Carol ...'

'And Phyllis cutting a hole in our ceiling,' said Noel.

'Yeh!' said Norrie. 'That was a *wild weekend*!'

'Pretty wild,' I said.

'Everybody in?' Trout hollered.

The bus started off, and we were on our way back to civilisation. Old Trout settled down on the seat beside Edwina.

He was looking pleased with himself.

I wondered what Edwina was thinking ... no I didn't! I knew what Edwina thought, she'd told me. And I could guess what was in Trout's mind. In the end, I was the one I was wondering about.

'Pretty wild!' Norrie repeated.

'Yeh,' said little Noel.

'Next year we'll really duff that place up,' Norrie said. 'If we go, that is.'

'Won't be the same, next year,' said Noel. 'We'll be older.'

I was concentrating hard on the back of Lorna's head.

She turned and looked back at me.

And she smiled.

A Selected List of Fiction from Mammoth

While every effort is made to keep prices low, it is sometimes necessary to increase prices at short notice. Mammoth Books reserves the right to show new retail prices on covers which may differ from those previously advertised in the text or elsewhere.

The prices shown below were correct at the time of going to press.

☐	416 13972 8	**Why the Whales Came**	Michael Morpurgo £2.50
☐	7497 0034 3	**My Friend Walter**	Michael Morpurgo £2.50
☐	7497 0035 1	**The Animals of Farthing Wood**	Colin Dann £2.99
☐	7497 0136 6	**I Am David**	Anne Holm £2.50
☐	7497 0139 0	**Snow Spider**	Jenny Nimmo £2.50
☐	7497 0140 4	**Emlyn's Moon**	Jenny Nimmo £2.25
☐	7497 0344 X	**The Haunting**	Margaret Mahy £2.25
☐	416 96850 3	**Catalogue of the Universe**	Margaret Mahy £1.95
☐	7497 0051 3	**My Friend Flicka**	Mary O'Hara £2.99
☐	7497 0079 3	**Thunderhead**	Mary O'Hara £2.99
☐	7497 0219 2	**Green Grass of Wyoming**	Mary O'Hara £2.99
☐	416 13722 9	**Rival Games**	Michael Hardcastle £1.99
☐	416 13212 X	**Mascot**	Michael Hardcastle £1.99
☐	7497 0126 9	**Half a Team**	Michael Hardcastle £1.99
☐	416 08812 0	**The Whipping Boy**	Sid Fleischman £1.99
☐	7497 0033 5	**The Lives of Christopher Chant**	Diana Wynne-Jones £2.50
☐	7497 0164 1	**A Visit to Folly Castle**	Nina Beachcroft £2.25

All these books are available at your bookshop or newsagent, or can be ordered direct from the publisher. Just tick the titles you want and fill in the form below.

Mandarin Paperbacks, Cash Sales Department, PO Box 11, Falmouth, Cornwall TR10 9EN.

Please send cheque or postal order, no currency, for purchase price quoted and allow the following for postage and packing:

UK   80p for the first book, 20p for each additional book ordered to a maximum charge of £2.00.

BFPO   80p for the first book, 20p for each additional book.

Overseas   £1.50 for the first book, £1.00 for the second and 30p for each additional book
including Eire thereafter.

NAME (Block letters) ....

ADDRESS ....

....

....